THE THEORY OF EVERYTHING EXPLAINED IN A SIMPLE WAY

Quantum Entanglement

Jack Veffer

ISBN: 9781081117733

ACKNOWLEDGMENTS

Thanks to my dear wife Catherine for her encouragement, her patience and her love.

Thanks to Dr. Ivan Samson and his dear wife Tony Samson for their wise counsel, understanding

TABLE OF CONTENTS

INTRODUCTION

The story of existence itself cannot exist without the Creative Force and the created. The innermost secret of life is that simple, an intimate relationship between the Creator and the created. Man knows what God knows. It is man's collective responsibility to learn and share. God's Knowledge and man's knowledge is entangled. Therein lies the explanation to the one theory that explains everything. What entangled means, in this concept, is that they are one and the same. Since we as human beings are constrained by time and space and even though according to the principle of entanglement we aught to know what God knows, so is our knowledge constrained by time and space. This means that we know it, but not yet. We feel proud with the knowledge of Einstein's theory of relativity. After all we are of the few that understand it. Why is it that in all this empty space we feel compelled to look for something? What drives us to do that? In his book 'A Universe from Nothing' physicist Lawrence Krauss explains: "Nature comes up with surprises that far exceed those that the human imagination can generate." He reminds us that our galaxy is one of 400 billion in the observable universe, and that star stuff and earth stuff are largely the same; that every atom in our body was once inside a star that exploded, a supernova. So our bodies are literally made of stardust. And all the structures we can see, like stars and galaxies were created by quantum fluctuations from nothing. Empty space has enough energy to dominate the expansion of the universe. Frank Close, professor of physics at Oxford University, in his book '*Nothing: A Very Short Introduction*' reminds us that an atom is a perfect void, 99.9999999999999 percent empty space. Its emptiness is profound. But it is filled with powerful electrical fields. A finite region of empty space having all matter removed will still be filled with energy and this energy fluctuates spontaneously, turning into electrons and positrons lasting only for 10 to the -21 seconds and fluctuating into and out of their virtual existence within one thousandth part of an atomic radius. Modern physics suggests that the universe could have emerged out of the vacuum. But Close concludes his book with the thought, "I am confronted with the enigma of what encoded the quantum possibility into the Void." *p.144*

IS A PARTICLE ALSO A WAVE?

Our comprehension of reality is caught up in experiences and the things that we see around us. If we can see something, it must be real. Without really understanding it, what also forms a part of our reality is the duality that exists between a wave and a particle: they are both considered as one and the same, and yet they are different. It is something we cannot readily see unless we look, not only with our eyes but also with our brain. How can it be one and the same? To compare it to something we know and understand we can compare it to water. Water can be ice or steam vapour and of course plain water. We have no trouble understanding that because we have grown up with it.

And so the duality really means the shape of matter where, sometimes it looks like a wave, and at other times it looks like a particle. Our everyday experiences of the reality we see around us builds our understanding, but more often than not we need someone to explain to us what it is that we actually are seeing. The wave-particle conundrum is so spooky that we are continually challenged to rethink our most common understanding of energy in motion. Our notion of reality is built on everyday experiences. The duality of the properties of matter is that at one time it acts like a wave and at other times it acts like a particle.

Why are waves so different from particles?
Particles bounce off each other while waves that collide, freely pass through one another and stay unchanged. Overlapping waves do interfere with one another but they overlap each other and some disappear altogether just like waves in the ocean.

The Uncertainty Principle.
Waves seem to be continuous but we're not so sure about the Particle. Where does it go? Well, we're not sure. We think it is somewhere in space. Where else would it be, right? This phenomenon is known as the Heisenberg's uncertainty principle. For ordinary everyday particles, like a baseball or a stone pebble because we can see them their location can be accurately measured unlike atoms or electrons, their location becomes less observable.

Einstein worried all his life about where the particle was located and since he could not come up with plausible answer he decided that valuable information was missing in the quantum theory. Thus Einstein and his colleagues Nathan Rosen and Boris Podolsky decided that there were two possible solutions:

1. The Quantum theory was wrong.
2. The problem resided in our notion of reality itself.

Eventually, through a series of experiments it was proven that the quantum theory was correct and that our understanding of reality skews our comprehension of reality. It is, however weird science, or "Spooky science" according to Einstein. Since particles always travel in pairs and no matter how far apart they are from each other, one meter or a million light-years they always feel each other. This is because of what is known as Quantum entanglement.

So what don't we understand about this? As Richard Feinman says: "Don't worry about it. Nobody really understands Quantum theory. Eventually we get used to the idea and we get on with our lives or some of us become philosophers." As far as reality is considered Richard Feinman put it this way: "The paradox about reality is the conflict between your feeling of what it is and what it really is. They are one and the same."

To explain the wave-particle duality I need to put it in a story

Once upon a time there was a wave and a particle. They didn't really know each other and they didn't really know that they were very much entangled. Entangled means a special way of being together, like knotted together in a knot: They play with each other and often are in the same spot at the same time but they don't know that they are very close to each other that they can always play together. The particles' name is Charlie and the wave is called Diana. Charlie was wandering around one day really not knowing where he was going and while he could feel that someone else was there, not his mommy or his daddy had ever told him what that meant. All he knew was that he could feel that somebody was there with him. They should have told him that when he and Diana mingle together, or when they share a closeness something happens that makes him feel happy and they can play together. What's really strange, he noticed, when they are very, very far apart from each other they can still talk to each other. Being so tied to each other makes Charlie feel good and no matter where he goes or how fast he goes, he somehow knows that Diana is with him.

The first time they met Charlie the particle laughed to the wave as he said: "My name is Charlie, what is your name?" The wave answered:" I am pleased to meet you Charlie and I have not just one name, I have many different names. You can call me Diana. We can hang out. We can play together and we can learn lots of things from each other. Do you think you would like that?" Charlie said: "I love to play games. I like to play games more than I like to do anything else. How about you?" "Yes I like to play too," said the wave "It's great to learn while you play.

Our notion of reality is built on everyday experiences. But wave-particle duality is so strange that we are forced to re-examine our common conceptions.

Wave-particle duality refers to the fundamental property of matter where, at one moment it appears like a wave, and yet at another moment it acts like a particle.

Do you know what it means to learn?" Charlie responds in a curious voice:" No I don't know what it means to learn. I have many friends and we all love to play together. Love to play. You know what's funny? I can't see you but I can feel you and I love to be with you even more than I love to be with my particle friends. Do you know why that is so?" "No I don't really know. Maybe it is because we are so different and yet we are also the same. I am you and you are me." Charlie says: "I don't get that."

"Diana, do you like me better than all the other particles you know?"

"Well I really like you a lot Charlie, but I like everyone else too. I haven't met a particle I don't like"

"But Diana we are the best of friends aren't we. Buddies for life, right?"

"Yes, we are Charlie. We need each other. Without each other we're not much."

"Why is that Diana?"

"Well Charlie it's like this. I am a wave and you're a particle. As the wave I make everything possible; what is, what was and what will be. But without you all that is of no use because you're supposed to learn all that knowledge and you are the one that has to make things happen in your life, not me. It is my job to give you all that you need to know to make your life happy and eventful and it is your job to learn it and share all that you know with all your friends. That's your most important duty."

"I don't understand what duty means, but that's OK. What game will we play?" an excited Charlie asks. After thinking for a while Diana answers:" Lets play a game called: LET'S SEE WHAT YOU KNOW." "What kind of a game is that? That doesn't sound like much fun," says Charlie in a pouting voice. "It will be fun, I promise, once you realize how important it is for your 'growing-up' as a particle. Let's try it and you'll see," says Diana.

"Ok, Charlie let's get started.

This is the first question: Why do you want to be my friend?

The second question is: What do you think we have in common?

The third question and probably the most important: "Can you make stuff happen? "Diana, I don't know the answers. Those questions are way too difficult for me. I would really much rather play games." "Come on Charlie: think! You probably know very well what attracted you to me." "Well if you put it that way then the answer would probably be that I want to be like you. Is that possible, even though we are so different?" Charlie asks "Very good Charlie. Yes, it is possible. At the same time that we are so different we are also very much the same. Charlie let me try to explain something to you before we can go any further; Even though we are different we are also the same. I am you and you are me. We need each other. Your mission in your existence is to know about me and to learn from me as much as you can. And that's why it is, that you as my friend, must pass on what you learn to all your friends, not that it matters to me whether you do that or not, but it will certainly matter to you and your kind. Without learning from me you will still be as you are, perfect in the way you are, but you will also, when you're ready to go on, be less prepared to go on your next big adventure when you're finished with your current adventure. We'll talk more about that later on. As a particle you have a very important mission: It's called "learning stuff". It is the part of you called conscious- ness and your consciousness always wants to learn new things. Consciousness is not only yours; it belongs to all of us. Together you and me can make things happen for you and for others. Always remember it and never forget it: As a wave I am the possibility but without you I am nothing. I can't make things happen on my own, but together we can make anything happen. That's why we need each other and that's why you and I like each other so much.

It's important for you to know that the choice to make things happen or not, is yours; it's called action. You use action when you play, for example. You have a unique capacity that is called "free will". That means that you can play anytime you want or not. My job is to show you things. Your job is to learn about these things and show others what you've learned. Together we are perfect and without each other you are not. I don't want to confuse you but when I tell you that I am a wave that is true but, and here comes the hard part to understand, there are many waves, too many to count. They are all me. Do you get that? So when you know me you can know all of me, if you want."

"I don't get that," answers Charlie, with a questioning voice. "Well you like stories right?"" Yes I do. ""Well if the story only contained one chapter and the chapter was interesting, then at first you would read that chapter over and over, but after a while you would grow bored and you would say what happens next. That is why a story has many chapters so you get to know what happens next and that is what makes the story more interesting. And so it is that you also have many chapters in your own story."

"Diana, you call me and my kind a species. What does that mean? What is a species and what other species are there? The other question I have is why do you act like you're the boss of me?"

"Smiling, Diana says:" Those are great questions Charlie. The type of particle you are is the kind that is curious; that can ask questions, the kind that wants to know everything, as you just demonstrated. You can do stuff and think about stuff and based on that you can make good things happen or bad things too, if you want. To better understand what I'm trying to explain let me put it in another way. Let's say that you are going to school. You know what a school is right? It's where you learn things. Ok well this school only has five grades. Grades 1 through 4. You can, because of the type of particle you are go all the way to grade 4 and beyond. These are the grades where you have learned to think and reason for yourself and lets you, based on what you've learned make decisions that can make your life more fun for example, eat the right kind of foods, drink the right drinks and sleep the right amount of time and live a happy healthy particle life and be part of a greater community with other particles that you like and are like you. You all live and play together. Ok so far?"

"I think I understand that Diana. What are the lower grades for?"

"They are for other kinds of particles that are not as smart as you. The grades are more like a category rather than the grades in a regular school. So for example you, who are in the highest grade, can see things that the particles in the lower grades cannot and will never be able to see. Just like you know that I am here with you, even though the image of me you cannot see because it is beyond your sight, nevertheless you know I'm here. A great benefit of your capacity, Charlie, is your ability to continue to learn things. So, you go from grade to grade always learning more. Never stop learning Charlie, because you also have to teach others what you've learned. The particles in the lower grades cannot see what you see and understand what you understand.

The particles in grade 1 for example, belong to the mineral world. These are the rock particles and the pebble particles and metal particles. They cannot see or understand what you understand. They just lay around all day quite happy because they don't have anything to do and they don't have anything to worry about. Now, the particles that are in the vegetable world that's another thing; they are in grade 2. The vegetable particles in grade 2 are smarter than the mineral particles in grade 1. They start out really small, as small as a seed and as time goes on, every day they grow bigger and bigger. That is one of their jobs; they have to grow into what they are meant to become. Some are to become an onion, a carrot, a kumquat or a broccoli, and one day they're really happy because they've fully grown into what they were meant to be; a potato or a carrot or an onion. So that's what they're supposed to do: grow and that's all. They can't talk or think like you. They have no feelings other than the feeling that they must grow. That is the sole reason for them to be here. No matter how big they grow or what kind of vegetable they are, they stay in grade 2 and they don't know and cannot see the animal particles, like you that are in grade 3. The fact that the vegetable particle is in grade 2 and despite his ability to grow and become what he is supposed to become; an apple seed will ultimately become an apple tree, or a potato seed will become a potato, or a pumpkin seed will become a pumpkin and so on, they cannot go to grade 3. There are many different kinds of animal particles and they know stuff about the rock particles and the vegetable particles, because they use rocks to play with and vegetables to eat. Animal particles have eyes and ears and other things so that they see the things around them and as I said they are in grade 3. Many have arms and legs and a nose to smell things with. Some are pretty smart animal particles like the monkey particles. They can climb trees and they enjoy the warmth of the sun as they lie about on a branch in a tree. They love their friends, the other monkeys. There are boy and girl monkeys and they love each other so that they mate and make other monkeys as a result of their mating. There are literally thousands of different kinds of animal particles. Some walk, some crawl like spiders, some fly like birds and insects and some slither like snakes. They can also see you and play with you like doggies for example. Some are called pets. Do you have a pet Charlie?"

"Yes I have a little doggie and I call him Buddy. I love Buddy and Buddy loves me. I take good care of him. I take him for walks and I brush his hair every day. I give him food and water."

"That's wonderful. We are supposed to take care of our pets. Even though some are in grade three many cannot take care of themselves and that is why you must take care of them. They are in your care from the day they are born to the day they die. They rely on you to show them things to do such as peeing outside the house and not inside. You feed them and you love them and you will soon see that all that caring pays off because they grow from a little puppy into a fully-grown dog. The particles in grade 4, like you Charlie are really lucky because they can see what is happening in grades 1, 2 and 3 and they have the ability to talk about it with the other friends who are in the same class. They can tell jokes to each other, like: What do you get when you cross a cow and a duck? Milk and Quackers! They can also tell stories to each other, like the story of Snow White. Or they can learn valuable things just by playing together. What's important to remember is that we all co-exist on this earth, each in the grade that we're assigned in and we must strive to be the best that we can be. The valuable lesson you must learn is that although *you* can understand what the rocks and the vegetables are, they cannot possibly understand you. Now here comes the hard part. I said that there are 5 grades and you and your other particle friends are in grade 4. Grade 4 lets you see the things around you with your senses. Do you know what your senses are Charlie?" Yes I do. They are my hearing so that I can hear the birds sing their tunes in the trees. I have ears so that I can hear my doggie bark when he wants to go out for a walk. I can hear the rustle of the leaves as the gentle breezes on a warm summers day blows through the leaves. I have a nose that lets me smell the wonderful smells around me and also those smells that are not so wonderful. I have fingers on my hands so that I can touch the potatoes that my mother wants me to peel for tonight's dinner.

"But Diana I am talking with you. Didn't you say that the particles in the lower grades cannot see the higher grades? So how is it possible that we can communicate with one another? By the way what grade are you in?"

"Charlie these are good questions and many have asked the same questions before you. The answer to the first question is quite simple. It is possible to communicate with me because you have something that is called imagination and that imagination allows you to see things that you can't really see with your five senses, but yet you see them with what you call your sixth sense. Your sixth sense is magical because although you cannot see, smell, touch, taste or hear me, you can imagine I'm here. You can imagine that I'm all around you. Imagination is the strongest sense yet since it allows you to see not only me but other things that are around you as well. Imagination is in fact the very ingredient you need to create a reality in your own mind that lets you see and do things that otherwise you could not see and do. It is the kind of reality that offers you hope when you need it or can make you happy again after you've been sad and love the things that are around you like your father and your mother and your new puppy. It is how you can learn about all the many things you did not know existed and through imagination all of a sudden they are there for you to see."

"As a wave I have always been here and as a particle you have not. You were born after something happened. It's called the big bang. Let me try to explain it better with a story: Once upon a time there were two particles one was a female particle and the other was a male particle just like you Charlie."

"Diana what are their names? Maybe I know them?"

"Charlie just listen to the story ok. Their names don't matter, right now, remember I said it was a story to explain the difference of you and me. Anyways they met and they fell in love and because they fell in love they came together and together they made another particle. So you see they made something happen and because of that happening another particle came into existence. Do you understand this story Charlie?"

"Yes I do, but how did they make another particle Diana?"

"Before I tell you that, you're going to have to learn much more than you now know. That is your mission while you are a particle in this life, you're living now, to learn and to use and to share what you learn. With this story I just wanted to show you what the difference was between you and me. Nobody made me, because I have always been here and since I have always been here, I simply know everything that happened before, that happens now and that will happen in the future and you and all the other particles are the ones that make these things happen. This makes me more like a teacher, if you will, not the boss. Particles are of this world you now live in and waves are in all the worlds. As a particle you happen to be a very smart one, in fact you belong to the group of particles that are the smartest of all the particles. You are a human particle. You can make things happen if you want to, or if you don't feel like it then nothing happens. It's all up to you. You know what that is called Charlie? It is called free will. You have free will, which means that as smart as I am and although I know everything I cannot make you do things unless you want to do them. So you see you are as important as I am but you still need to learn as much as you can. I can teach you but I can't make you learn if you don't want to learn. More importantly, that which you learn, you must teach to the other particles. That I can't do for you either. So you see Charlie we are both equally important."

"Guess what Charlie. After you pass from this existence as a particle, you go into your next existence and then we can see each other much better. I may be like you; say the boss of you, however it is much more important that you realize that we need each other. If I know everything, that knowledge is of no importance without you. That should make you feel important. All the knowledge that there is does not mean anything unless you do something about it by sharing it with everyone else."

"What does that mean Diana?" asks Charlie with a surprised look.

'It means that without you doing something, nothing happens. We must share our experiences with others. I can show you stuff and you have to show that stuff to other particles. Without that, knowing stuff and never using or sharing it is pretty useless."

"It makes me happy to know you Diana. I don't need any other friends. You show me everything I need to know."

"I like you a lot too Charlie."

"Diana I was wondering about something. When I was looking for a name to call you, you said that you had many different names and also that you were not only one wave but that you were all waves. I don't understand. Can you explain that to me?"

"Ok, one thing at the time. Your first question about my names: The answer is quite simple. Particles cannot see me but they know I'm there just like you see me. Since I don't talk to every particle they come up with their own names for me that is why I have so many."

"I had a question for you Diana. I know that as a particle I am pretty small and that my friends the other particles can only see me. But you can't be seen at all. How can I better see you?"

"Good question Charlie. You can only see me through actions."

"What does that mean?"

"Maybe I can explain what I mean through an example. I know you're pretty small but let's say that if you pick up a pebble and toss it in a pond you will see a wave because the pebble moves the water. That is how you know that something has happened. There are many different kind of waves: sound waves, radio waves, micro waves, electro-magnetic waves, electrical waves, ultraviolet waves, x-ray waves, gamma-ray waves and many other kind of waves…. When absolutely nothing happens all the waves are at rest and they are just straight lines. That is called equilibrium, and as soon as one thing happens then one of the waves out of all the waves becomes a wiggly line. That's how you know the difference. Many things go on at the same time all the time. So many things happen at the same in fact that the number is not countable. There are so many waves that can make things happen that someone called it "the field of unlimited possibilities" (Deepak Chopra)." There are waves that you can see, such as the waves of the ocean. They are big waves. And then there are many waves that are so small that you can't see them or hear them. There are waves you cannot see but you can hear them like radio waves. There are waves you can neither see nor hear but you know they are there like electricity waves."

"What is this field of unlimited possibilities?"

"Let me see if I can explain it with an example; there once was a particle and his name was Ernst Schrodinger. Ernst had a box. He also had a cat and he put the cat in the box and he closed the lid on the box. He left the box for a while and then he wondered if the cat was alive and having fun in the box or maybe his cat was no longer alive but dead in the box. Yes Charlie I know it's a cruel thing to leave a cat in a box. Schrodinger left the cat in there for a while and he said to himself, until I open the box I have no idea if my cat is alive or dead so the only thing I can think is that the cat is both alive and dead, until I open the box and then I will find out that the cat is alive or dead, but until then the field of unlimited possibilities that Deepak talked, in this case only 2 possibilities, is that the cat is both alive and dead is true. Any possibility is true until you personally see it.

Another example of the field of unlimited possibilities is that if a tree falls over in a big forest but you're not there to hear it fall the question you have to ask yourself is if the falling tree makes a sound?"

"Of course it makes a sound Diana."

"Are you sure of that? You're not there to hear the sound. The best you can say is that there is a chance that the falling tree makes a sound or maybe it does not or maybe it both makes a sound and it does not make a sound at the same time. Again we are talking about the field of unlimited possibilities. It's only when you're there to observe that you know for sure. And that is the reason why you're so important to us Charlie. I can't tell others about what you see and hear but you can. You are my eyes and ears. All that I can do is to show you and teach you things and your part is to tell others what you see and hear."

"I think I get it Diana. You are a wave and I know you're there because I can talk with you and I can hear you, right? I can see you do things because when you do things your straight line becomes wiggly."

"Yes sort of like that. My wiggly or straight line can be compared to a straight string or a wiggly string. I am everywhere around you and also in you. Your imagination is the place where you can imagine things. It's a very important place. It's the place where you can discover and imagine things that you did not know existed before and all of a sudden your imagination tells you that they are there. Sometimes they are not there though. So you have to find out the difference. That is why it is important for you to learn about things so that you can become smart enough to know the difference. You can make things happen if you want. That is called intention and intention is very important for you and for your friends. So you see we need each other. You need me and I need you. Not only can you make things happen or discover new things you can also tell others about these."

"Diana, I am really tiny now, I know that, but can you tell me what I will be in time when I grow up?"

"Charlie, what you are right now, even though you are small, is perfect and what you will become depends on what I call your destiny. That destiny has been pre-determined for you. What you will actually become you can control. You can strive to be the best that you can be, whatever it is."

"Who decides what I will be when I'm grown up?"

"You decide Charlie, Circumstances and your will determines that you will be what you're supposed to be and I can help you because one of the other names they've given me is "The Universal Will". The Universal Will is the name that tells you that I can help you to be what you want to be, but it really is up to you; what you want to be.

You can make things happen Charlie. You and Me are energy and you have a special part to play in what is called the energy of life. The energy of life has blessed you with some important powers, one of which is consciousness and the other is reason. Your consciousness ties you and the other particles together so that each of you, when you are in sync can feel the same things. You can share these things for example if you feel happy you can share that feeling with all of your friends, the other particles. They do the same for you. If on the other hands all the other particles feel sad and they make you feel sad too, you can actually think about your sadness: why you feel sad. What you can do about you're feeling sad and how you can change your sadness into happiness. That is the reason part of your energy. You can say to yourself: Self I don't want to feel sad. I can make myself feel happy by thinking happy thoughts: The sun is shining, the birds are singing, I am happy. This way you turn your sadness into happiness."

THE ENTANGLEMENT BETWEEN GOD AND MAN AND THE THEORY THAT EXPLAINS EVERYTHING

I n the Talmud, the subtle relationship between the individual reflective mind (man) and the universal consciousness (God), as reflected in the dialogue between Abraham and God, went something like this: God says to Abraham: *"If it weren't for Me, you wouldn't exist."* Abraham *thoughtfully replies, "Yes, that's very true Lord. I thank you for that. But, if it weren't for me, nobody would know about you."*

Both together are necessary for one another. The story of existence itself cannot exist without both participants. The innermost secret of life is that simple, an intimate relationship between the Creator and the created. Man knows what God knows. It is man's collective responsibility to learn and share. God's Knowledge and man's knowledge is entangled. Therein lies the explanation to the one theory that explains everything. What entangled means, in this concept, is that they are one and the same. Since we as human beings are constrained by time and space and even though according to the principle of entanglement we aught to know what God knows, so is our knowledge constrained by time and space. This means that we know it, but not yet. We feel proud with the knowledge of Einstein's theory of relativity. After all we are of the few that understand it. Why is it that in all this empty space we feel compelled to look for something? What drives us to do that? In his book 'A *Universe from Nothing*' physicist Lawrence Krauss explains: "Nature comes up with surprises that far exceed those that the human imagination can generate." He reminds us that our galaxy is one of 400 billion in the observable universe, and that star stuff and earth stuff are largely the same; that every atom in our body was once inside a star that exploded, a supernova. So our bodies are literally made of stardust. And all the structures we can see, like stars and galaxies were created by quantum fluctuations from nothing. Empty space has enough energy to dominate the expansion of the universe. Frank Close, professor of physics at Oxford University, in his book '*Nothing: A Very Short Introduction*' reminds us that an atom is a perfect void, 99.9999999999999 percent empty space. Its emptiness is profound. But it is filled with powerful electrical fields. A finite region of empty space having all matter removed will still be filled with energy and this energy fluctuates spontaneously, turning into electrons and positrons lasting only for 10 to the -21 seconds and fluctuating into and out of their virtual existence within one thousandth part of an atomic radius. Modern physics suggests that the universe could have emerged out of the vacuum. But Close concludes his book with the thought, "I am confronted with the enigma of what encoded the quantum possibility into the Void." *p.144*

We can only conjecture. We know that what is termed empty space in the universe or 'Void', as Dr. Krause refers to it, is far from being empty. It is energy that is simply not discernable to us in its present state. Because we can't see it, does not imply that it is not there. If you assume or believe in the possibility that something exists can you explore the possibility of its existence? In that way, we can conceive that the universe—and possibly anything else outside of the universe—may in fact seethe with energy identifiable as virtual particles and antiparticles that erupt spontaneously into being. These are contained in dimensions that we are unaware of presently. These new discoveries may provide answers to some of cosmology's most fundamental questions: what lies outside the universe, and, if there was once nothing, how did the universe begin? Then, of course, we can always fall back on the Higgs boson, the building block of the universe, the so-called 'God Particle.' The boson itself provides the necessary proof for the existence of the Higgs energy field. We can liken the Higgs field and the boson particle to electricity and the light of a lamp.

We don't know what electricity is but we see its evidence in the light it creates. If you see the light then you know that electricity exists. So for the boson particle to be there, you know that the space for that particle is there too. So it is with the belief in God, that to know the existence of God, we can observe God's qualities and attributes in the utterings of His Prophets. Since the Higgs particle was observed at the CERN lab in March of 2012, we're pretty sure that the Higgs energy field exists.

PURPOSE

One important aspect of living completes the mission we have been given to fulfill while in this life and that is **PURPOSE.** It is the centerpiece of our life on this earth. If we listen carefully we are given guidance and rules to live by. All organisms must abide by that guidance. These rules and guidance are so critically important, in fact, that as we grow smarter as human beings they are continually updated and the purpose for our existence becomes ever clearer. We are born "tabula rasa" that is, without the knowledge of what the rules are. You might ask how do we know that we are born for a purpose to fulfill? The answer, it seems, is because if we were just born without that mission to fulfill, we would be born without the ability to reason, without the natural curiosity, without free will, without the ability to pro-create, without feelings of empathy, generosity and most importantly without the ability to feel love for one another. What the next question is that comes to mind is 'why are some people born bad' and without some of those feelings? The answer is simple; the attributes of love, compassion, empathy, curiosity, generosity...are listed under the heading of knowledge or light. If people do not have these attributes they live in darkness or the absence of light. To remedy that, we can turn on the light; in other words we can teach them.

Five different kinds of capacities in the universe drive the organisms inhabiting the earth.

The first capacity is vegetable. It is the ability to grow like vegetables grow. All created things starting with vegetables, animals and humans have the ability to grow. Growing is their only capability without really being able to figure out other things from nature.

The second capacity is animal. It is the capacity to grow like animals. All animals including humans have the ability to grow. This capacity includes perceiving our surroundings with our senses: sight, smell, touch taste, hearing. It lets animals be empathetic.

The third capacity is human as well as some of the higher animals in nature. It is the capacity to grow like humans grow and allows us the power of reasoned thought. It is made up of the noblest most perfect composition of all existing elements in the universe.

The fourth capacity is spiritual. This capacity is strictly a human capacity. It is the ability to uncover the healing power encompassing all things. All the qualities that do good, all the wondrous discoveries, all the mighty under-takings and significant historical events of which we become aware are discovered by this spirit and revealed to us from an invisible source into our consciousness. We humans residing upon the earth are enabled to make heavenly discoveries and make magnificent deductions that benefit humankind in this realm. For example, our bodies are heavy and yet we find ways to fly through the air like birds. We are slow and we devise ways to travel at the speed of sound. Man's power encompasses all things.

The fifth capacity is heavenly. This is the capacity that humans do not possess and is the ability set aside for the few appointed through the power of the creative force and who counsel us on things to come. This is the reviving spirit that is conferred upon us by these stain-less mirrors who counsel us on the changes that are the divine springtime for humanity.

Chief Tecumseh, a Shawnee chief's poem was featured in a movie called "Act of Valour" it exemplifies senti-ments on man's mission in life:

> *So live your life that the fear of death can never enter your heart. Trouble no one about their religion; respect others in their view, and demand that they respect yours. Love your life, perfect your life, beautify all things in your life. Seek to make your life long and its purpose in the service of your people. Prepare a noble death song for the day when you go over the great divide.*

Always give a word or a sign of salute when meeting or passing a friend, even a stranger, when in a lonely place. Show respect to all people and grovel to none.

When you arise in the morning give thanks for the food and for the joy of living. If you see no reason for giving thanks, the fault lies only in yourself. Abuse no one and no thing, for abuse turns the wise ones to fools and robs the spirit of its vision.

When it comes your time to die, be not like those whose hearts are filled with the fear of death, so that when their time comes they weep and pray for a little more time to live their lives over again in a different way. Sing your death song and die like a hero going home.

~ Chief Tecumseh (Poem featured in the movie: Act of Valour)

IS THE MIND A PART OF THE BRAIN?

An automatic answer to that question is: "Yes, of course it is. The mind and body are the recipients of the sum total of all knowledge. So it is evident that all your cells are the benefactors of all the same knowledge and experiences that your mind possesses. They can and do continually communicate with each other. Your body, having started out with the union of two cells, is comprised of approximately 100 trillion cells. The knowledge is imprinted in every single cell of your being. The ability of your mind is in its capacity to function as a standalone, complete unit and is the mirror image and storage unit for everything your brain processed in the past, the present and the future. The mind retains that information forever. It is like the disk drive of a computer. Your brain communicates with all the parts in your body and vice-versa, and is the integral part of who you are and how you function and can be compared to the "central processing unit (CPU) of a computer. Your mind stores all the information, required for your body to keep functioning while you are alive and in this body.

[The Mind is] an embodied and relational process that regulates the flow of energy and information, consciousness included. Mind is shared between people. It isn't something you own; we are profoundly interconnected. We need to make maps of we because we is what me is. Daniel J. Siegel, 1999, The Developing Mind, p. 3.

William James used the term 'transcendental mind,' a continuum of cosmic consciousness that exists in a higher dimension and subsumes individual minds. The Catholic theologian, Pierre Teilhard de Chardin, posited the existence of a membrane of consciousness encircling the globe that would be enhanced anytime the consciousness of any one individual in the world is raised. Leonard Shlain writing in Art and Physics goes further and describes the universal mind as an over-arching, disembodied universal consciousness that orga-nizes the power generated by every person's thoughts. Shakespeare said it well, when he had Macbeth lament while he was praying *'My words fly up, my thoughts remain below. Words without thoughts never to heaven go.'* We are a part of a much larger entity existing in the space-time continuum with an agenda we are not aware of yet. The individual self-reflective mind knows that it knows, but the universal mind knows everything, everywhere and anytime. Everything we experience, every memory, emotion or thought is part of that process, not a place in the brain! That is what is meant by 'embodied,' as in 'contained' or 'part of.' Relational means that it is related to something. So it means that we are all part of the process and we're all connected. So the process is being able to do something or use energy in other words. There's nothing that is not energy; even mass is energy. Remember E=MC squared? Hence, the mind is an embodied and relational process (action) that regulates the flow of energy and information.

POTENTIALITIES INHERENT IN MAN

We have been endowed with the faculty of vision, the power of hearing, a sense of smell, the capacity to feel through touch and taste. These powers have given us the ability to discover the palpable potential of our destiny on earth and the innate perfection of our reality. Wonder if there is such a thing as heaven? What it looks and feels like? If there is a Heaven what, if anything, must we do to get there? These and many other questions are answered in this book. Read on and get ready to be amazed by the simplicity of the discovery of it all. In order to enjoy the full potential of the discovery of a Heavenly destination and our place in it we must first acknowledge the signs of God. This acknowledgement is the distinguishing feature of every Godly belief, and at the very core of our spirituality. Upon it depends the commitment of all goodly deeds. The acceptance of a heavenly place must be difficult to accept without also accepting, at the same time, a perfect unifying essence that makes the place perfect. If we can identify heaven without also accepting its perfection we say that the place is not perfect. That is impossible; it is like saying that darkness is light. Both conditions cannot exist simultaneously. If you cannot recognize this

Divine principle you have not yet attained this most lofty place and uncertainty will confound you. Once you have embraced it, this teaching will deliver you from all manner of doubt and let you embrace salvation in all the worlds of God.

THE SOUL'S POWER

A good question to ponder is whether man, after his physical death will retain the self-same consciousness, personality, and individuality. Gaining an understanding of what characterizes man's life in this world is fundamental in answering this even though death, which includes the decomposition of his body and the dissolution of its elements, cannot destroy that understanding and extinguish that consciousness, even when the very instruments necessary to their existence and function will have completely disintegrated, how can any one imagine that man's consciousness and personality will be maintained without changes; even when the lack of his mental faculties will deprive him of understanding his own consciousness and his death? It is therefore natural to assume that man in this new bodiless existence will have to attain to a different kind of consciousness, one that involves the acceptance of a different much broader awareness.

It is an individual's obligation to be a witness to the unfoldment of the progressive revelation of God's Knowledge. The acquisition of knowledge is of paramount importance for the soul's progression into the next world of existence. To be sure, that is not all that's required, because the acquisition of knowledge is merely one step in a two-part process. The second step is the application of that knowledge for the common good. What compels us to do His bidding? We need to add love, a special kind of love that includes the close ties you have with others, such as your parents. This love is binding. It is usually the type of possessive love that makes you feel cuddly, warm and safe that you belong. It is a nurturing love that also contains a strong social component. It makes you feel that you are an important part of the human family. When you cultivate that love, it must include the qualities of love, compassion, equanimity and humility.

Is it that very essence; that indefinable energy that separates truth from untruth, wisdom from error, or is it the One that possesses all the knowledge, and is it He who urges us to share all that we know with others? We are incredibly unique, in a galaxy of billions of stars we live on the one planet that has produced intelligent life, as we know it. Our planet can sustain this life and make it better by us helping to share some of the things we have learned since its' fiery start. We have evolved from a single cell with a simple existence to a multi cell organism with the ability to perform complex tasks and not only can we make sense of our existence we can also make sense of the universal matrix. As we evolve into smarter and smarter beings we have the capability to replicate many of the building blocks of our own creation. We are capable to reproduce our own kind, not only in the way we were ordained to do but also by duplicating the components that make us, in the lab from scratch.

We have to first acknowledge that God's essence is the all-encompassing energy responsible for all that occurs in the universe and to whose promptings we all abide. After that acknowledgement we are then ready to do our share for the advancement of the wellbeing of all the things that are within our realm of responsibility. This then is what we have been told by the enlightened souls who have been imbued by the essential guidance, the Essence we spoke of before. At birth we have all been assigned important tasks. We can accept these tasks or ignore them, since as part of our creation we have also been given free will. There is a serious effect that if we chose to ignore our responsibilities, to share this universal knowledge with others, we also need to prove to ourselves that we are not part of the destiny of man and what it is that really motivates us into action. Aside of the lack of help in providing answers for the universal fulfillment of man's destiny we must be able to justify our inaction, not in this life but in the unfoldment of destiny once we've left this earthly existence. Can we deny that there is no knowledge beyond that which we currently know? No we cannot! If the universal consciousness resides somewhere, who is the keeper of the knowledge? We have been given clues. Throughout life you will be called upon to figure out things with the most cryptic of hints from the creative force. Try to always be mindful of the progressive unfoldment of the universal knowledge and don't be discouraged if at first you don't get it. Remain steadfast and keep searching since it is the most important enterprise of your short existence on this earth. And even if you encounter derision or ridicule keep your eye on the prize for it is what you learn and share with others, in this life, that will result in a fulfilling afterlife with your gaze firmly fixed on the Sun of Reality, the greatest reward for a life well-lived.

Earthly experiences are created both, through the five senses, and in the brain from a myriad of sources: imagination, the result of previous experiences, logical deductive reasoning, past historical events and metaphysical expectation. Most of that which, we use as our inspiration for the progression through this earthly life is already existent in the universe of knowledge and is passed on from those with whom we interact, such as family and teachers or interaction with other individuals or events. This knowledge and experience is used to make up our own earthly reality. Liken it to being the director and writer of your own movie. We have a collection of picture frames put together in our own minds and this adventure of ours is uniquely our own creation and no other movie from anyone else in the universe is quite like ours. No other animal in the universe has this capacity to forge its own story as it travels through this physical existence. Why is that so? Because human beings have a free will. We have the capacity to make things go one-way or the complete opposite way, all based on the independent decision-making power we posses. Each individual experience is "space-related" and unique and reserved. So this leads us to the conclusion that each human story is in its own reserved space in the space and time continuum. Since the space and time continuum must reserve space for all conditions, it makes sense that whether a condition is fulfilled based on our own decision, the space for its alternative must also be reserved, just in case you change your mind. The paradox of space if you decide to take it to its inevitable absurdity: What has always been logical to me is that everything that has mass occupies a space in my universe. I does not matter what the mass is; a football, an apple, banana, a kumquat, human body, a whale, that space needs to be there otherwise the mass cannot exist. With that concept in mind what space holds the universe? The space itself; mass, has a mass, if not at least it must have a volume and then the paradox sets in, in that the volume itself occupies a space which must be contained by another space and so on… ad infinitum and that makes no sense at all. Therefore there must exist another solution to this conundrum. Let's try to see if the space occupied by the singularity before the big bang, occupies a space? Wait we must have a vantage outside to see the singularity. That's impossible if everything is within the singularity there can be no outside vantage point, except in our own minds so it cannot be a reality so it's our imagination that can only contemplate this event. There is a moment in time when we are not witness to events and we must accept anything that occurs until that time and before that time as something that is true, except we can't prove it. It is called a metaphysical truth.

It leads one to the inevitable conclusion that we are not talking about just one universe but multiple universes. Stephen Hawking refers to this phenomenon as "multiverse".

And so while we're in this life, in this body, we learn and we learn through the five senses. From a practical perspective, in this timeline, we are beyond the stage that we do harm to ourselves because we've learned not to and because we aught to know better and nevertheless, we still harm others and ourselves on a daily basis. That is paradoxical and the disadvantage of having a free will. We learn not to blow ourselves up by making the wrong decisions. We have a built in sense of self-preservation by learning right from wrong decisions and all that experience (knowledge) as are all our decisions saved in the large pot of knowledge, named as the universal subconscious by Carl Jung, and this subconscious knowledge can be used by anyone else in the multiverses. We have our five bodily senses and in addition the brain power that takes advantage in learning, right from wrong, good from bad, harmless from harmful and thus we put our experiences to work for the good of all, not necessarily because we are altruistic but for very practical reasons. By living together with others we do well not to blow ourselves and others up, we learn for the survival of all and put into practice, practical and common sense actions that are of benefit to us and thus a benefit to all. One generation of existence builds upon the ashes of all previous generations that came before it, gathering knowledge as we evolve. All the accumulated knowledge is mixed in with the knowledge that is yet to be discovered by man. In other words all knowledge is already made available and accessible to us either through man's cumulative discovery of this knowledge or through discovering new knowledge by listening for queues provided by forces yet unknown to us. It becomes more and more evident to us, what our mission in our bodily existence is. It is, at once, for our own education, so that we can travel through this existence equipped with all the knowledge that is available to us and also to make this knowledge available to others, by teaching it to those who are interested. We must be cognizant of the fact that there are forces arrayed against us to prevent us from sharing this knowledge because the individuals are on a different journey. I've come to the inevitable conclusion that while in this reality made up of dust and blood and other stuff we are here with a mission to fulfill. We are proxies for a greater entity or we are avatars or we are parasites. It's not likely that we are parasites since we have a free will and we don't operate through instinct alone. So either we are proxies here to represent the needs of that greater entity or we are here, as avatars living out the life of the greater being with a destiny, but also with an autonomous will.

There is another field of thought in relation to living out our earthly existence without the guidance of a Greater Entity. There are two ways to view life.

We can contemplate life on this plane in at least two separate ways.

1. Metaphysically, and with the responsibility to serve the needs of the One God, or Greater Entity...
2. Without the knowledge of a God. Just as an entity with a mission to optimize our own comfort and that of those we love on earth.

A QUANTUM EXISTENCE WITH A
METAPHYSICAL DESTINY

What is metaphysics? How can we refer to something we don't know exists or does not exist? What is the nature of reality? How does the world exist, and what is its origin or source of creation? Does the world exist outside the mind? If things exist, what is their objective nature? How can the incorporeal mind affect the physical body? Is there a God or many gods, or no god at all?

Metaphysics was derived from the Greek word Metaphysica, a word that means beyond physics and was later redefined by Aristotle as the study of "It is what it is and it transcends physics". Metaphysics is that part of philosophy that deals with abstract subjects, like the Singularity, time, space, being, knowing, first cause, identity, substance. It is an abstract theory with no basis in reality. It is, in fact, reality that is not discernable to the senses and a challenge to most of us who believe in something that we cannot see or feel and yet, somehow we are fascinated by the thought of something invisible that is greater than us and existed way before our existence. It doesn't leave us alone as if we're drawn to it like a magnet. It is the unshakable belief that a Creative Force made us into who and what we are. Aristotle split the study of metaphysics into three sections:

- Ontology, the science of being and existence, both physical and mental. The nature of being, and the nature of change.
- Theology or the study of God. The nature of religion. The acceptance of a divine will. Questions about our creation, and the various other religious obligations and spiritual issues.
- The Universal Science, the study of First Cause and the law of non-contradiction.

Continuous existence is self-evident and its meaning does not need to be proven in order to be true since, it is a prerequisite for the acquisition of knowledge. It follows that we cannot deny it, since denial would simply mean that existence is "nothing" as opposed to "something" and that is counter-intuitive. So it follows that our consciousness is the ability to contemplate and recognize things that exist. René Descartes stated that consciousness goes without saying, simply since you cannot deny the existence of your mind (the place where consciousness exists) while at the same time use it to do the denying.

What Descartes left unclear in his dissertation is that consciousness is the one faculty that recognizes that which exists, so it needs the ability to perceive things outside of its own self: it is that very essence we call existence and that existence is the very first thing and that consciousness is secondary to that existence. Without existence we cannot be conscious and consciousness does not create reality it is completely contingent on it.

To exist in this contingent world we are ensconced in the reality of time and space and a metaphysical existence is not a part of time and space, it is beyond it and therefore not definable and yet there is a strong feeling that it exists. We accept its premise as a part of the origin of man as well as a part of man's ultimate destiny after our life ends here on earth. It is an abstract notion with a strong degree of veracity even though we are not able to prove it.

If it is true that we are all created, we're nevertheless "blank canvasses" upon which the creator has left his indelible imprint. Nothing that is really discernible but more like a "paint by numbers" canvas; the connecting points are there, and the colours are already chosen. We, each of us, need to connect the dots and transpose our colours of life upon our own canvas. Our unique canvas will almost certainly differ in colours and hues, representing our work of life in progress. Each canvas is a unique masterpiece. We are made up in the most beauteous tones and shapes of such exquisite design that when we contemplate it, it makes our soul skip a beat. Sometimes the colours and shapes are tainted by the harshness and disconsonance of the rhythm of life, but if we let life's experiences unfold in full colour, we can make our own masterpiece the best that it can be. As a full participant in the universal subconscious, we have unfettered access to knowledge, and it is up to each one of us to discover it, to share it and to incorporate the good to influence our life with the voice of good reason and good moral judgment.

The Singularity is known by many names, God, the Source, the Creator and because it came before us its' essence is not knowable to us; all that we can perceive of the Creative Force's essence is through the attributes that are manifested to us by His appointed Messengers, Abraham, Moses, Zoroaster, Mohammed, Baha'u'llah, and many others. These appointed individuals are truly his stainless mirrors reflecting His qualities as if they were God Himself. Some of the qualities they manifest are love, tolerance, empathy, justice, orderliness... in short all those qualities that allow us to live together in love, harmony, justice and unity. His truth, not always self evident, is true now and forever. This truth is latent in the universal subconscious. All we require to accept God's truth is faith; it's that simple but also that complex if you don't believe in the entity of a God. Without faith we can never understand God. Once these have been turned on, they will remain turned on as part of our personal thumbprint, our conscious guide and become part of what makes you at once unique and alike in the human experience. This universal truth is less self-evident for those who do not believe in a

God. They too can evidence these attributes by observing those with a god-fearing attitude; just don't give it a label.

Everything you are; your personal make-up, your character, your physical body, your mental body, your personal well-being, sickness or good health has its origins in your brain and your gut and finds a permanent residence in your mind. Make no mistake about it, your brain and your gut impact on everything you are and everything you do. You can't turn it off. Through experimentation we've discovered some important aspects: if your brain is the central processing unit of everything you are and do, your mind is the repository (like a hard drive) and it can affect you in a most positive way and conversely affect you in a most negative way. That is why it's so important to know and understand your brain and how it makes you function. It is like being your own psychoanalyst. People spend great amounts of money trying to figure out what makes them tick. It's a billion dollar industry.

In order to be a success in life and in order to feel good about yourself it is imperative that you get those good qualities out of your head (we all have them) and into your life where they can do some good.

We have patterns in life that provide guidance, based on this universal consciousness and act as blueprints for the training of the soul. These patterns of life are:

1. The divine pathways: time and space. Embrace it for eventually it will all make sense.

2. The divine proportions: the exquisite, divinely ordained patterns of aesthetics and form that make traveling along the path of life a delightful experience. We also listen to god's (the divine architect) who gives us our guidance for the proper migration of the soul into the next existence, after we've departed from this earthly life. Thus the mind laden with the sum total of all revealed knowledge, the universal subconscious, accompanies the soul upon passing into the next world of existence. It is that knowledge, and the application of that knowledge for the common good, that lets us progress towards the "light". If we did not adequately prepare the soul during our earthly existence it will limit our ability to get closer to that "light". It does matter how well we prepare our eternal soul in this lifetime. Carl Jung, said that: "I simply believe that some part of the human self or soul is not subject to the laws of space and time." (Carl Jung, quotations.). Our life is a work in progress, an adventure orchestrated by a force that unerringly guides us on a journey of discovery and if we listen very carefully it will allow us to live a rewarding, wholesome, soul satisfying existence. Learning, acquiring knowledge is key to achieving this, and by embracing it we can live every day of our life the way it was meant to be.

In a TV interview, quantum physicist Fred Alan Wolf said, with respect to consciousness: "I feel like we're on the verge of a gigantic discovery - maybe the nature of God, maybe the nature of the human spirit." he also described a "global consciousness in which what one being does affects everyone on the planet."(*Fred Allan Wolf, Towards a Quantum Field Theory of Mind*)

Ultimately we must realize that logic alone may not provide us with all the answers and that a healthy amount of faith is a necessary component in solving life's mysteries. Consciousness exists in a dimension that we know exists but not yet know where or what it is. I've called that dimension, the divine dimension that like the soul is not physically connected to the human frame and yet is an integral part of our being while we are here. So out of necessity, we need to listen to the metaphysical qualia to help define its nature.

A question that is crucial to spiritual wellbeing: Is the heart the seat of the soul? Baha'u'llah, the Prophet Founder of the Baha'i Faith, answers the question unequivocally "O My brother! When a true seeker determineth to take the step of search in the path leading unto the knowledge of the Ancient of Days, he must, before all else, cleanse his heart, which is the seat of the revelation of the inner mysteries of God, from the obscuring dust of all acquired knowledge, and the allusions of the embodiments of satanic fancy. He must purge his breast, which is the sanctuary of the abiding love of the Beloved, of every defilement, and sanctify his soul from all that pertaineth to water and clay, from all shadowy and ephemeral attachments." *Baha'u'llah, Gleanings From the Writings of Bahá'u'lláh, p.264*

We think with our brain and we feel with our heart. Where then is the mind? The brain goes through a progressive evolutionary process and continually evolves biologically. Consequentially, when we think that the mind, wherever it is located, creates everything, we talk about experiences and conscious awareness and not necessarily complicated thought. So the definition of what the mind is, is still being hotly debated. Yet, the mind is a conscious experience and is a divine mystery. Theories abound. Some maintain that the mind functions because the brain is only a biological computer with the ability to process algorithmic functions only, while the mind and consciousness are non-algorithmic, involving feelings and sound and colours... The brain with its billions of neurons, neurotransmitters, proteins and synapses works because of its super sophisticated electro-chemical system. The mind works in conjunction with the brain in its capacity to store the information, make it uniquely yours and finally, it has the unique ability to consciously and thoughtfully execute your richly textured information. If the mind has been properly trained it does so in an elegant, common-sense-aware manner imbued with some or all of the God-like qualities we learn, love, empathy, gentleness, truthfulness... and incorporate these in our everyday life to make it the beautiful work in progress that it is. In addition to these important functions, the mind is the repository for the sum total of all the experiences of the soul. Language is infused with references to the heart and feelings of tenderness, sadness, happiness, emotion and state of mind. It causes us to look at the heart for the softness and gentleness and altruism and all else that is good and seemly in us all that "tempers the wild beast", while the brain drives us to heroic, logical and methodical actions. The heart doesn't think though and yet it is the heart that causes us to cry when we see the suffering of others and even though it does not think like a brain it impels us to perform acts of incredible kindness without guidance from our brain. How does it do that? We're all key players in the gradual, progressive unfoldment of the universal consciousness, as evidenced by the use of this discovery in the unfoldment of a kinder gentler world if we are so inclined. We certainly have that capacity now.

Our soul is unique to us and it hungers for development. We can teach others but we can't share our soul with anyone else. The independent search for knowledge and the maturation of our soul is an individual pursuit that draws on the resources available in the universal subconscious and the day-to-day learning of truth while we are alive. The results of this acquired knowledge is continually tested in the application of this knowledge for the common good. If it makes others as well as ourselves better then we are on the right path. If we cause pain to another, it is the heart that is affected. If our dear ones are sick or incapacitated it is the heart that hurts, and the grief or trouble of the heart will adversely affect the body's wellness. When we find truth, constancy, fidelity, and love, we are happy; but if we meet with lying, faithlessness, and deceit, we are miserable.

There are things pertaining to the soul that do not cause bodily ills. Thus, it is apparent that the soul has its own individuality and if the body undergoes a change, the soul is not touched. When you break a mirror on which the sun shines, the glass is broken, but the sun still shines! If a cage containing a bird is destroyed, the bird is not harmed! If a lamp is broken, electricity still flows!

"The same thing applies to the spirit of man. Although death destroy(s) his body, it has no power over his spirit—this is eternal, everlasting, both birthless and deathless." *Abdu'l-Baha, Paris Talks, p. 66*

"As to the soul of man after death, it remains in the degree of purity to which it has evolved during life in the physical body, and after it is freed from the body it remains immersed in the ocean of God's mercy." *Baha'u'llah, Gleanings From the Writings of Bahá'u'lláh p.324*

From the moment the soul leaves the body and arrives in the world of the spirit, its evolution is spiritual, and that evolution is the approaching unto God.

"Yet in the physical world, evolution is from one degree of perfection to another. The mineral passes with its mineral perfections to the vegetable; the vegetable, with its perfections, passes to the animal world, and so on to that of humanity. This world is full of seeming contradictions; in each of these kingdoms (mineral, vegetable and animal) life exists in degrees; though when compared to the life in a man, the earth appears to be dead, yet she, too, lives and has a life of her own. In this world things live and die, and live again in other forms of life, but in the world of the spirit it is quite otherwise." *Abdu'l-Baha, Paris Talks, p. 77*

We are given the soul at conception. It is an everlasting soul that lives forever. It is also unique. It does not grow like a plant would grow, but rather it matures. What you do with it will determine where the soul will actually, not physically, be after it leaves your body. Finally, the soul is pure energy, not matter.

The ongoing debate continues over who or what is responsible for the origin of the universe, although science and religion are integral parts of the world of existence and each have played distinct and important roles in piecing together parts of the mystery of the universe, man's search speaks of a universe that expanded from "the initial singularity", a point of infinite density from which the big bang occurred, to an unending vastness of unfamiliar objects scarcely dreamed of just a century ago. Man's search has not been limited to looking for answers in the sciences, but also involves searching in the realm of the divine.

Throughout his history, man has arrived at many different conclusions about how we came to be. We have hotly contested which of the two, evolutionism or creationism is right. Advocates for the two theories have competed fiercely. Now it appears evident that the two are collaborating in order to understand our origins.

In the divine dimension, and passing through the divine gateway where we embrace the divine proportion we contemplate neither the reason nor the purpose for actions and phenomena as it shows us an exquisite glimpse of divine form and divine substance in a divine rendering, an integral part of the universal subconscious. What has preoccupied man since we got up off our knuckles, is the beginning and the common thread linking us all. Beginning with the innocence of a child: "mom why is the sky blue?" To Stephen Hawking: "God if all knowledge comes from you and all knowledge is in all of us, give me the key to the theory that explains everything." To Fibonacci who said: "I discovered numbers that explain the face of god." To Mozart:" I hear the sweet voice of God and I'll put it to music." To Leonardo da Vinci:" I see God. I think I'll paint him." To Vincent van Gogh:" I can smell god's divine fragrances, I'll paint some flowers." To Shakespeare:" God speaks to me and this is what He says." To George Gershwin:" I hear God's music and this is what it sounds like." To Jesus the Christ:" God I see Your Perfection and I'll die for it." To you and me:" God I know what needs to be done. Today I'll do it better than I did it yesterday." The idea is that we've all been touched by something so sublime, so exquisite as to make of us all wide-eyed creatures with an insatiable lust for knowledge. Go for it; don't let life's tribulations stop you. Ask questions. Go out and help someone feel good. Be full participants in life. Be your own life changer. The only impediment to change is in your own mind.

Our conscious thought is what controls everyday life, but it is "what we know that we don't know", in our universal subconscious, that can make all the difference. It is a place that lets us tap into the unlimited knowledge. Our ability to tap into it and the way it animates us will govern how much or how little we progress spiritually and thus becomes a measure for the attainment of perfection. What then are these circumstances? We don't know for sure. What is sure is that we can learn better in some mental states than in others. It is therefore important to zero in on that most perfect condition that maximizes the learning process and enhances physical and mental wellbeing. Unfortunately in most of us the aspiration for attaining excellence remains forever dormant. All of us are irresistibly drawn to the universal consciousness; our mind and our soul are an integral part the whole."

We must ask ourselves whether our creation was an accident or was it pre-ordained? Paradoxically, it probably was both and now that we are here we are part of the destiny of existence, to perfect ourselves just as we were meant to do. There are rules in life of which we need to be aware. One of them is to discover who we are; the second rule is to know where we fit into the scheme of things. Another is to discover where and how we fit into the universal consciousness. In the primacy of this consciousness how do we participate in the dignity of the progressive unfoldment of our destiny? So it is that the Universe came into existence replete with all that is and all that will be; that includes all the knowledge and all the witnesses to this knowledge, including us. Since we are witnesses to knowledge with the ability to share with all other existences, we are the primary conscious mouthpieces for the discovery of knowledge, in this existence anyway.

So if it is true that we are witness to the unfoldment of the progressive revelation of God's Knowledge then we're also compelled to do His bidding. It is that very essence; that indefinable energy that separates truth from untruth, wisdom from error, and He is the One who possesses all the knowledge, and He who urges us to share all that we know with others. We are incredibly unique, in a galaxy of billions of stars we live on the very one planet that has produced intelligent life, as we know it. Our planet can sustain this life and make it better by us helping to share some of the things we have learned since its' fiery start. We have evolved from a single cell with a simple existence to a multi cell organism with the ability to perform complex tasks and not only can we make sense of our existence we can also make sense of the universal matrix. As we evolve into smarter and smarter beings we have the capability to replicate many of the building blocks of our own creation. We are capable to reproduce our own kind, not only in the way we were ordained to do but also by duplicating the components that make us, in the lab, from scratch.

We have to first acknowledge that God's essence is the all-encompassing energy responsible for all that occurs in the universe and to whose promptings we all abide by. After that acknowledgement we are then ready to do our share for the advancement of the wellbeing of all the things that are within our realm of responsibility. This then is what we have been told by the enlightened souls who have been imbued by the essential guidance, the Essence within. At birth we have all been assigned important tasks. We can accept these tasks or ignore them, since as part of our creation we have also been given free will. There is a serious consequence if we chose to ignore our responsibilities, to share this universal knowledge with others; we also need to prove to ourselves that we are not part of the destiny of man and what it is that really motivates us into action. Aside of the lack of help in providing answers for the universal fulfillment of man's destiny we must be able to justify our inaction, not in this life but in the unfoldment of destiny once we've left this earthly existence. Can we deny that there is no knowledge beyond that which we currently know? No we cannot! If the universal consciousness resides somewhere, who is the keeper of the knowledge? We have been given clues. Throughout life we will be called upon to figure out things with the most cryptic of hints from the creative force. We must, therefore be mindful of the progressive unfoldment of the universal knowledge and not be discouraged if at first we don't get it. Remain steadfast and keep searching since it is the most important enterprise of our short existence on this earth. And even if we encounter derision or ridicule we must keep our eye on the prize for it is what we learn and share with others, in this life, that will result in a fulfilling afterlife with our gaze firmly fixed on the Sun of Reality, the greatest reward for a life well lived.

In this life we, the people of this earth, are the mouthpieces of God. How did we receive this daunting task? What does that mean, exactly? For some reason we find ourselves, the most highly evolved creatures, at the center of creation with the unique capacity to not only uncover all the knowledge we need to exist in this life but also with the capacity to uncover all the knowledge; that which we need and that which we don't need in this life. We also have the ability to be witness and share this knowledge with all the other organisms in the universe. What a responsibility that is and one that cannot be taken lightly or with the idea that someone else can do this for us all and we get time off to enjoy all the frivolous things life has to serve up. Let's face it there are enough distractions for a lifetime of inertia. That is, however, not our purpose in life. We need to ask ourselves why it is that we have been bestowed with the capacity to observe all that the universe offers up and then also have the capacity to tell a story about it. Not only through the five senses but also by interpreting what we think we've observed, like hearing a new song and liking it or reading a new book and disliking it. It's a strange thought to think that the God, or the Creative Force or the Supreme Force or whatever you chose to call it does not communicate Himself in a clear voice about the mysteries of existence. He does, you say, so how is it that not everyone hears Him.

Our role is to acquire God's knowledge. It would have been far easier if we had not been designated with the unique capacity to observe and tell all. Like the other living organisms they experience what we experience and in a certain measure are able to form an opinion because the instincts they are born with compels to the next step: your pet tells you he's hungry and barks so you can get him his food and after he's satiated he brings you his leach so you can take him for a walk. How clever, you think, my dog's a genius, but why can he not tell you in a clear voice that the earth is round and not flat? Because he has the ability to observe through his five senses, as we do, but lacks the capacity to interpret that information and to come up with an entirely new idea about what he saw and to share this new idea with the rest of the world. Since we have that capacity our duty is to share God's knowledge with others. So we're the ones on this earth who understand our mission and who are actively engaged in providing knowledge to all living things.

"God, your name is my very being and being aware of you is my wellbeing. Being close to you at all times is my eternal wish and my deep love for you is my comfort now and forever. You are truly all I need, for you are the One who knows all and who is all."

EXISTENCE WITHOUT THE BELIEF IN A GOD

To attempt to gain an appreciation of life without a God we must look at the writings of Nietzsche, a German philosopher and cultural critic and the quintessential atheist. He and Kierkegaard were considered the starters of a movement called existentialism. His writings on consciousness, on morality and the meaning of existence have had a profound influence on Western discourse.

His famous, oft repeated quote, "God is dead. God remains dead." was the very statement religionists needed to start the debate about the existence of God for, they maintained that since He is now dead he must have been alive at one time. It did not matter that Nietzsche himself proclaimed, that it wasn't what he meant when he uttered the statement. Some students of

Nietzsche believe that he embraced nihilism, an argument he himself denies. It is a viewpoint that stresses that normal-everyday-values and beliefs are unfounded and that existence is senseless and useless. He rejected philosophical reasoning, and endorsed a literary exploration of the human condition, while also rejecting a metaphysical acceptance of a greater entity than us. Passing on that which we learned was not a prerequisite to gain entrance into heaven since there is no heaven and therefore no need for us to learn and pass on anything. However, those who accept Nietzsche's teachings say that he wished to engage in a positive programme to redefine his view on life, by affirming that the nature of human existence, and the attributes of knowledge and morality are basically noble and purposeful for their own sake and not necessarily as a stepping-stone for entry into heaven. It is generally accepted that he suggested that "becoming what one is" through the cultivation of instincts and various cognitive faculties, is a plan that requires a lot of effort given what we've inherited from our parents and surroundings with regard to intellectual and psychological capacity.

He stated that man's need to realize an exemplary human condition stems from his own desire to be the best that he can be without the need to do so to be in God's good graces, or for the perfecting of a soul. He did not view eternity as a gateway for the recurrence of events. Nietzsche did espouse a cosmological view on "will to power" (the ubermensch) as the driving force for man to be the best that he can be. Nietzsche did concede that the decline of religion and therefore the absence of a higher moral authority would cause chaos in the world. This statement caused several of his existentialist colleagues, Albert Camus and Jean-Paul Sartre to reply that the need for a higher order was an absurd notion since man had no need for a higher authority. Other philosophers were less inclined to completely part with the idea of a higher authority and tried to introduce a concept of an absolute morality man adheres to without the need for a supreme entity. The final outcome of the argument is still unresolved and will remain so until we get confirmation from the other side one way or the other.

WHAT IS THE MIND?

The mind is not something we own, it is something we share. In the metaphysical world many things are inter-connected so when we speak of the mind we must ask ourselves what it is? [The Mind is] an embodied and relational process that regulates the flow of energy and information, consciousness included. Mind is shared between people. It isn't something you own; we are profoundly interconnected. We need to make maps of we because we is what me is. (*Daniel J. Siegel, 1999, The Developing Mind, p. 3.*)

Leonard Shlain, US surgeon, inventor and a best-selling author explores the potential for humankind through the lens of the life, the art, and the mind of the first true Renaissance man, Leonardo da Vinci. In his book Leonardo's Brain the author explains what da Vinci's enormous body of work will achieve in the future.

Da Vinci's inventions were truly impressive and as an artist he had no equal. Shlain tries to explain, through contemporary neuroscience, that da Vinci's creative process was way ahead of its time. Although there have been many genii throughout history, that stood out for their genius, no other person has excelled in so many different areas of innovation: Shlain attempts to show the how and the why of Da Vinci's genius. Shlain theorizes that Leonardo's extraordinary mind came from a uniquely developed and integrated right and left-brain and offers a model for how we too can evolve. He uses past and current research, as a guide to explain.

Leonardo's Brain presents da Vinci as the focal point for a fresh exploration of human capacity. Shlain brings the reader into the world of one of history's greatest minds. Ultimately we will all of us have the same capacity Leonardo Da Vinci had even though Leonardo had it way before anyone else. Eventually through some kind of brain enhancement, that will be available to us in the very near future, we will all have a far greater brain capacity.

CONSCIOUSNESS

CONSCIOUSNESS IS OUR REALITY.
Rene Descartes, centuries ago, started the debate about consciousness:" Je pense, donc je suis (I think therefore I am)". It is foundational to the debate, not that anybody will argue the statement today. It is, however, a narrow-minded view of how the universe, with us in it, functions. Philosophically, we're still trying to determine whether consciousness ends at earthly demise or whether it's a dual reality consciousness, dividing it into earthly stuff and mind stuff. It now appears that neither is true and that through a greater understanding of modern neuroscience we've embraced a more pragmatic approach, guided by a greater understanding of the philosophical arguments that promotes a continuity of consciousness, at once endless and seamless transcending time and space. It's not really necessary to understand the philosophical arguments why consciousness

exists and is seamless, it is more important to accept it to use it as a bridge to accept its continuity. Consciousness is our reality. Its reality transforms both scientific and medical understanding. Encouraged by the positive outlook, countless scientists are now studying this idea as they feel it might be closely related to the nature of our reality. It's our perception of this living world and our thoughts and intentions about it, our awareness of the things around us, and so on. We're all interconnected.

The answer is more than trying to grasp the philosophical argument; it takes the collaboration of philosophers, neuroscientists, cognitive scientists, psychiatrists, brain imagers, mathematicians and computer virtual reality experts and together we are gaining new insights into consciousness, providing new answers into the field of medicine which yield new intellectual and ethical challenges. The ongoing research provides new insights in how the brain and the body co-operate, revealing a picture in how conscious experience is deeply rooted in the brain and the body to maintain physiological and spiritual integrity. The understanding is a two-part challenge; the first one is easiest because it consists of how the brain learns and behaves, perceives and recognizes. The second part is to grasp why it is so important that we need to learn to do all those things; why can't we just be like zombies or robots, where we just do without questioning? What is the reason we're trying to solve the mystery of consciousness? It's to attempt to figure out how it affects the wellbeing of all living organisms. Why is consciousness important to our health and wellbeing?

Collective consciousness is continually updated. It's functionality shifts as time evolves and we become smarter. The time has come for all of humanity to work towards the greater good for all. There is a new awareness that changes the collective needs of society and there can be no excuse for us here in the Western world, living our comfortable lives, for example, to continue in a mode where we remain blissfully unaware to the needs of others, when the rest of the world lives in poverty, violence and destruction. We are not innocent bystanders any more; we must become the agents for change. So the more people we can engage in changing complacency into action, the quicker we can effect the changes necessary for the betterment of the destiny of man. It is the primary reason why we need to continually update our knowledge, so that we can be the agents for changing all of humanity for the better. Thus you must always learn new things. Knowledge is both progressive and cumulative. The knowledge of life is freely available to us all and is stored in the mind and the mind, with all its secrets, will be released together with the soul; at the moment the body dies. The mind can transport us to a greater vision, and it is stored, for its universal use, in the collective subconscious. The mind, by the way, is not to be found in any one particular place: It resides everywhere in the body, in the brain, in the heart, in the vital organs, in your muscles, in your limbs, in the top of your head and the tips of your toes. Being able to gaze inside the mind for subtle Divine Guidance and inspiration, with its inherent qualities of empathy and love, will give us the ability to study the inner reality and purpose of life. Without it we consider the external world to be the sole reality of life. Meditation frees the mind from the external world while allowing it to concentrate on the deeper meaning and at the same time, developing the capacity to find solutions for life's problems from within. Meditation requires freedom from distractions and lets us become aware of our inherent potential.

The mind replete with the output of our life's experiences can find the responses to our "creative questions" in the answers that were provided for us by those that came before us. The prophets, manifestations of the Creative Force, provide testimony, at length, to a spiritual interpretation of our impulses. From a practical aspect those impulses can be utilized in our physical state to provide the bulwark for an orderly society. It is an ever-evolving process. As our physical presence matures through the application of our creative knowledge, these are then used to provide for the needs of this maturing society. It is a communal, cumulative spiritual maturation that allows us to become more familiar with the spiritual progression of the path towards "The Eternal Light."

Thoughtful insight is rarely crystallized in a frenetic mode. On occasion we must permit ourselves to be quiet and contemplative. It is in those rare moments that we find essential verities that facilitate understanding of the mysteries of life. Noise diverts our attention and quietude lets us concentrate. Now, the mystery about noise is that certain wavelengths or frequencies are in a range that, even though we know they are present, cannot be perceived by humans. So it is therefore permissible to presume that time itself, except for the present, is in a frequency range that is not "inhabitable" by humans. When I refer to time I do mean the entire time spectrum, past, present and future. We can interact with time in the present but we are incapable to interact with time in the future or the past. I find that strange and I feel that it won't be much longer until man finds the key to unlock past and future time that will let us be active participants in these time frames. We already conjecture that we can do this when the soul leaves the human frame and itself becomes an integral part of the energy spectrum. Information is bits of knowledge and knowledge in action can be viewed as waves, or energy in other words. When we attempt to construct an image of these waves in some meaningful manner we can also display them as graphical information such as in the design of buildings, resulting in a three-dimensional rendering that demonstrates the economy of the inner-space we're trying to create.

I remember that, as a child I looked for the disembodied voice in the radio fully expecting to see a little person there. Imagine my disappointment when I saw nothing but lights. No one explained to me how that could be so. Little did I know that my brain, because of what it had learnt so far, whenever it heard a human voice, expected it to emanate from a person. That was its reality and anything else was too confounding until I learnt different.

So important was the idea of consciousness that scientists John Wheeler and co-author Wojcieck Zwiek stated:"It was not possible to formulate the laws of quantum mechanics in a fully consistent way without reference to consciousness". *J.A Archibald & W. H. Zwiek, Quantum Theory and Measurement, p. 169 Princeton Legacy Library.*

Eugene Wigner, theoretical physicist and mathematician commented that the idea that consciousness creates reality might be true but sounds farfetched, for it raises more questions than it answers. Does it mean that we can shape and create whatever reality we'd like for ourselves? Does it mean we can create our own lifestyle both individually and collectively and therefore attract our own experiences? Is its occurrence instant or does it take time and how much time does it take? How do we do that? Can anybody do it?

Even though we can't answer these questions with certainty we strongly suspect that a correlation exists between the physical material world and consciousness. We also conjecture that this consciousness cannot end when the physical material world ends, upon death and that it therefore continues forever. Our knowledge is still so limited.

Studying the new physics together with the epigenetics biology lets us postulate that in fact we do create our own reality. It's an irresistible attractive thought. Pioneering physicist Sir James Jeans wrote: "The stream of knowledge is heading toward a non-mechanical reality; the universe begins to look more like a great thought than like a great machine. Mind no longer appears to be an accidental intruder into the realm of matter. We ought rather to hail it as the creator and governor of the realm of matter. Let's get over it, and accept the inarguable conclusion. The universe is immaterial-mental and spiritual." *James Jeans, The Mental Universe, Nature 436:29,2005*

Now that we know all this, how can we use this valuable information and make it part of who we are and use it to transform our universe? For sure, it needs our participation and we need to transform in order to incorporate this new awareness of our being. Buddha so wisely said: "We are what we think. All that we are arises with our thoughts. With our thoughts we make the world." *Gautama Buddha, Dhammapada*

Nikola Tesla, the great inventor, was greatly influenced by Vedic philosophy and used it to help him to crystalize his ideas about quantum physics when he pondered his ideas of free energy or zero point energy. He said, and I am paraphrasing, that the universe works best when science and spirituality are in harmony. He conjectured that we could utilize the substance that exists all around us and convert it into usable energy, giving us a limitless source of energy. Many others like Newton, Einstein and Descartes shared similar notions. Why, do you ask, is all this of importance in a book on quantum thought? Because we are finally discovering that we as observers and participants in the universe are also shaping our own reality. What we observe and what we think has a profound impact on our lives and the lives of those around us. Most of us think that we are merely passive participants in a world we cannot control and all we do is pass through life without causing a ripple. The most important challenge we have is to raise a family, find a job and try to stay out of trouble the best way we can. What we should be doing instead is to become agents for change and create a new reality for us and for the rest of the universe, based on the very things we've learned that is rooted in hope, love and unity. Obviously, knowledge is the key. When this new knowledge is applied it changes the way we perceive things and as a result our reality changes with it. Classical as well as quantum physics, in complete unity, without opposing each other together with a positive sense of spirituality, will help generate this reality. That also means that the change must come from within us. Is our perception of the external world a reflection of our inner self? I think it is. We can test it by asking ourselves questions:

Am I happy? Am I loving? Am I angry, spiteful or hateful? These questions and many more like them, will determine your emotional state and help you to observe life from a happy, loving, positive place rather than from an angry, hateful, negative place. Don't forget that it's a work in progress, as was mentioned before. We are, all of us the observers as well as the observed and if most of us change our consciousness, from a sad place to a happy place, we will positively impact our life on this earth for the betterment of all humanity. Corny as it sounds, but true nevertheless; "Be the change you wish to see in the world." *Mahatma Ghandi*

At one time biochemists did not believe that biology could ever prove the properties of being alive. That is no longer so and even though our understanding is still incomplete they no longer doubt biology's ability to explain life. By explaining the properties of living systems' underlying mechanisms: reproductive, homeostasis, metabolism, etc... we've learned important lessons about life. Consciousness is singular, that has no plural. The reason for that is simple. We are all connected, through action, circumstance and knowledge. Being aware is not your exclusive domain; you share what you know and what you experience with everything else in the cosmos. That is the uniqueness of being. So when you explore the purpose of your being by attempting to find out who you are and what defines the unique you, you quickly determine that you are not so different; you are more the same like everyone else than different from everyone else. What sets us apart one from another are the circumstances that lead us into different directions. It is the path of life that shapes us into who we are. It is perhaps dichotomous that we have an exclusive responsibility for the development of our unique soul, and we all have one, while at the same time bearing a common responsibility for the development of the "common soul" of humanity. Every action we undertake and every bit of information that is gathered is done for the education of our soul and for the good of all. The soul, when the time comes, laden with the information it has gathered is ready to enter its next existence: enter the black hole and meet the singularity within. I think it is appropriate to define the destination that is the black hole. It is the same location as that which we call heaven, the metaphysical definition of the same destination called "entering heaven". I think that, if everything in the cosmos is referenced as energy, no matter if it is made up of elements now, we can follow the ultimate destination of all.

If you accept that everything is made up of energy it makes sense that eventually, all energy winds up in the same place, wherever that place is. It needs to satisfy certain rules, however, before it can enter. The rule is simple: The energy is all spent and it has reached a state of equilibrium, or conversely that the energy can no longer be used by its present user, which means that, although there is residual energy, the owner is no longer "alive" to use it. Yes the place has many different names but it is the same place.

The common universal consciousness is an integral part of the Singularity. The Singularity itself is that essence that many "God-fearing" people identify as the God-principle and others, although they don't believe in God, identify as intelligence greater than their own intelligence and therefore, outside the human sphere of comprehension. No matter what we believe we accept it for what it represents; knowledge that cannot be explained or as Aristotle said; "It is what it is."

Consciousness also, even though it cannot be explained, emanates from that same singularity. It is what animates us. It is that part of the human experience that makes us "God-like." So when God "made" man in His own image he gave us the ability to be like Him which gives us the capacity to be God-like in our interactions with others. We don't necessarily understand it, but we can use it in our daily actions. It does not identify the essence of consciousness but it demonstrates the inherent qualities. No matter how we analyze the brain we cannot discern consciousness. It cannot be defined just like God (Singularity). We cannot comprehend its essence (what is it?) but we can see its attributes or sentiments like love, hate and empathy and we can recognize consciousness by looking at ourselves in the mirror. Reality is like that: We see ourselves so therefore we exist. That's not all, since our consciousness needs to be defined by human sentiments as I said before, these are sentiments that give us the qualities we discern as the very consciousness for which we have no words."

Why is it that we can only accept, God's existence ontologically and without having any proof of His existence? The answer is simple, because God's essence is energy. We cannot see energy but we know how to use it and because we know how to use energy we know it's there. Although consciousness in this life is made up of only those things we can define and those things are made up of biological knowledge, we can still embrace the existence of a God. The reason we comprehend it here because our Biology is a science that requires order and logic. Those are things that do not necessarily identify God. In our next existence, after this bodily existence, we will be in that space and we expect that we might be witness to that essence we call God. It is a world of existence that is not ordered through biological events and that existence will be random and without order, but it won't be chaos.

Consciousness is singular that has no plural. The reason for that is simple. We are all connected, through action, circumstance and knowledge. Everything that affects you affects everyone. Being aware is not your exclusive domain; you share what you know and what you experience with everything else in the cosmos. That is the uniqueness of being. So when you explore the purpose of your being by attempting to find out who you are and what defines the unique you, you quickly determine that you are not so different; you are more the same like everyone else than different from everyone else. What sets us apart one from another are the circumstances that lead us in one direction or another. It is the path of life that makes us who we are.

Now, the mystery about noise is that certain wavelengths or frequencies are in a range that, even though we know they are present, cannot be perceived by humans. So it is therefore permissible to presume that time itself, except for the present, is in a frequency range that is not "inhabitable" by humans. When I refer to time I do mean the entire time spectrum, past, present and future.

We can interact with time in the present but we are incapable to interact with time in the future or the past. I find that strange and I feel that it won't be much longer until man finds the key to unlock past and future time that will let us become active participants in these time frames. We already conjecture that we can do this when the soul leaves the human frame and itself becomes an integral part of the energy spectrum.

Consciousnes

Consciousness is the universal awareness that we collectively gather and the mind is thus the custodian of all the knowledge for the benefit of all else in the universe and is the most important notion we come away with.

The story of energy, spirituality and sharing attempts to demonstrate that no matter how existence and consciousness is perceived, it is part of the universal energy in all its countless forms, at work for the good of everything in the universe. Through this lens we observe the unlimited number of dimensions representing existence. Action and intention formulate the path our life takes as we participate in the universes' unfoldment. Through action we become participants in our own destiny so inaction leaves its unfoldment to random chance. We can't leave our life's unfoldment to others since it will skew the outcome. Participation is key because the wrinkle we generate in the fabric of the space-time continuum is a space uniquely reserved for us. This reserved space is all-important and so it is that in the universe any event or energy, whether it is in the past, present and future does not or cannot exist if the space for that event is not reserved. When we think of being in charge of our own destiny we are responsible for making these events occur, as they are competing with many other events in the field of unlimited possibilities. Everything in the universe is pre-destined to happen or not. We are an integral part of our own destiny and by gaining the knowledge necessary for its best outcome we are instrumental to the best unfoldment of our own existence. The outcome of events is a result of our own actions. That is the free will part of our life. Inevitably we are confronted with the results of our own actions

One of the most praiseworthy traits in a person's character is Righteousness.

Education is the key to the soul's development.

Man is the only entity, which we know of, who is made up of two distinct and separate identities, the body and the soul. When the soul is ready to detach from the body, the body devolves into nothingness, so that the soul can detach itself and attain the speed of the Universe and become embraced by the limitless world of the hereafter; where neither time nor space can impede our contemplation of all the worlds of existence. Each soul is unique. Your rational soul is linked to your mind. It is an entity, at once part of you and yet separate from your body. Your body is the conveyance, like an automobile, and your soul is its passenger, with you as the chauffeur. Where you go and where you actually wind up is a conscious decision that you as the driver in charge must make. The soul has no control. The universal subconscious provides you with knowledge that allows you to make choices. You've got the answers in your mind; you must know the right questions to ask and determine which the correct answers are. You are in charge here. Your soul is immortal. It contains everything that is intensely, unequivocally and irretrievably you. It is "born" with you at your very conception and it is everlasting. It must be educated. It learns. It is capable of receiving good and evil alike. It cannot discern one from the other. Another similarity between the soul and the embryo is that the child must develop his limbs and organs in the womb of his mother. If he is born without some of these, he will be handicapped, for he is unable to acquire them in this life. The soul too must develop spiritual qualities in this world. The acquisition of wisdom, knowledge, love, humility and all other divine attributes is possible only in this earthly kingdom. We note that some limbs or organs seem to be useless in the womb-world. For instance, eyes are incapable of seeing there, but when the child is born, the light will bring vision to his eyes. The combination of the two—eyes acquired in the womb, and the rays of light existing in this world—endow a human being with vision. "Similarly, the virtues and perfections which the soul has acquired in this world, combined with the conditions of the spiritual worlds which are unknown to us while on this mortal plane, will cause the soul to progress in the next life." *Adib Taherzadeh, The Covenant of Baha'u'llah, p.9.* But your mind knows the difference. Your brain digests, dissects, analyses, ponders and then leaves it up to your mind to decide what becomes appropriate for the education of your unique soul. The choice is yours to make.

Through education and experience we can educate the soul. Mistakes are reversible. Your brain and your soul, work in harmony to do good or evil in this terrestrial life.

We make the choices. We model ourselves after others. Familial patterns of behaviour are often emulated. We can't seem to help it. If we witness patterns of violent behaviour in our parents, chances are that we will emulate these patterns. If alcoholism is a problem with our parents there is a chance that we will inherit these traits. Consciousness and a cultivated moral judgment will often correct disconsonant models of behaviour. The broader our education is, and with a discerning mind, we can break the cycle of propagation of negative models in our life and thereby mitigate the impact they have on our soul.

In our eternal soul's next existence, it will not be constrained by time or space. Everything exists at once and is observable at once. You can dwell in one part of space and at the same time observe a different part that is billions of light years removed from your point of observation. The soul that was uneducated, during our bodily lifetime, will have great difficulty in seeing this. The education of our uniquely personal soul begins while we are alive and needs to be readied to experience a seamless progression into the next existence. Everything here on earth is slowed down, finite, with boundaries shape and size. We observe most things as matter here. In the next life it's all energy and all that we observe is really a soup of electromagnetic energy and even though our soul remains unique we are all an integral part of the soup. The memories of our experiences here, in this life, serve as pillars of recognition in the hereafter.

When the soul is ready to detach from the body, the side that is released first is the logic side so that the soul can slow down and become introduced to the limitless world of the hereafter where neither time nor space play any role in our contemplation of the world of creation.

From a metaphysical perspective the soul's journey, in its travels to discover its "Maker", goes through seven distinct stages: The stages according to Bahá'u'lláh are described as search, love, knowledge, unity, contentment, wonderment, poverty and nothingness. Some extracts are shared below:

1. Search and its quality is patience
2. Love and its quality is purity
3. Knowledge and its quality is tireless purpose. "Split the atom's heart, and lo! Within it thou wilt find

a sun…" *Baha'u'llah, The Seven Valleys And the Four Valleys, P. 17*

4. Unity with its inherent quality of oneness and its rallying cry: "all songs are from the King." *Baha'u'llah, The Seven Valleys And the Four Valleys, P. 18*

5. Contentment with the quality of boundless understanding. "And we have made thy sight sharp in this day." *Baha'u'llah, The Seven Valleys And the Four Valleys, P.31*

6. Wonderment and its quality of astonishment. "Thou comest from the world of holiness—bind not thine heart to the earth; thou art a dweller in the court of nearness—choose not the homeland of the dust." *Baha'u'llah, The Seven Valleys And the Four Valleys, P.33*

7. Poverty and Nothingness. Poverty as here referred to is being poor in the things of the created world and rich in the things of God's world. "These journeys have no visible ending in the world of time, but the severed wayfarer—if invisible confirmation descend upon him and the Guardian of the Cause assist him—may cross these seven stages in seven steps, nay rather in seven breaths, nay rather in a single breath, if God will and desire it. And this is of "His grace on such of His servants as He pleaseth." *Baha'u'llah, The Seven Valleys And the Four Valleys, P.40*

Introspection is great, but brain activity includes all matters of reception and communication. The ability to think a thought, digest it and verbalize it to others is a perfect exercise for mental acuity. Without the capacity for the verbalization of your ideas, your brain loses part of its potential. As we age we tend to become more introspective. That is not necessarily a bad thing. It is said that with age comes wisdom and part of that wisdom is the way in which we receive information and the way we play it back. In aging, however, our brain becomes less active, less elastic if you will. That is why it is so important to train yourself and that your brain remains active. Your brain needs exercise, just like your body needs exercise.

The universal soul is always acting upon your personal soul for your entire life. The universal soul is the first cause, the outside voice acting upon our soul. The celestial (not of this world of existence), perfection, the incorruptible and it, will educate your soul and your mind if you let it. This voice of good reason and good moral judgment that is resident in the universal subconscious, attempts to continually engage us. Let's explore some of them.

You are a newborn baby and your mother is hugging you as she feeds you, turns on your collective subconscious and awakens feelings of possessive love. You are loved and your soul responds in a cognitive and positive way.

Most of the time we only trust our senses; that which we can see, hear, taste, smell or feel. God's essence, being unknowable, is forever hidden from our eyes; all that we can perceive of god are his attributes as manifested to us by the messengers god sends our way from time to time.

They truly are his stainless mirrors reflecting his qualities as if they were god himself. His truth, not always self evident, is true now and forever. This truth is latent in the universal subconscious. All we require to accept god's truth is faith; it's that simple. Without faith we can never understand god's verities. Once these have been turned on they will remain turned on as part of your personal thumbprint, your conscious guide and become part of what makes you at once unique and alike in the human experience.

Your immediate surrounding is an exaggerated mirror image of your brain. Those things that surround identify the intensely, personal individual you. Your soul is affected by the sequence of events in your life, by your family, father and mother and siblings, by your friends and your teachers. Sometimes an outstanding individual or a kind act can leave an indelible mark upon your soul.

Everything you are; your personal make-up, your character, your physical body, your mental body, your personal well-being, sickness or good health has its origins in your brain but finds a permanent residence in your mind. Make no mistake about it, your brain impacts on everything you are and everything you do. You can't turn it off. But hold on there is good news: if your brain is the central processing unit of everything you are and do, your mind is the repository (like a hard drive) and it can affect you in a most positive way and conversely affect you in a most negative way. That is why it's so important to know and understand your brain and how it makes you function. It is like being your own psychoanalyst. People spend great amounts of money trying to figure out what makes them tick. It's a billion dollar industry.

In order to be a success in life and in order to feel good about yourself it is imperative that you get those good intentions out of your head (we all have them) and into your life where they can do some good.

We have patterns in life that provide guidance, based on this universal consciousness and act as blueprints for the training of the soul. These patterns of life are:

1. The Divine Gateways: time and space (mandalas)
2. The Divine Proportions (The phi ratio). The exquisite, divinely ordained patterns of aesthetics and form that make traveling along the path of life a delightful experience.

The mind laden with the sum total of all revealed knowledge, the universal subconscious, accompanies the soul upon passing into the next world of existence. It is that knowledge, and the application of that knowledge for the common good, that allows us to progress towards the "light." If we did not adequately prepare the soul during our earthly existence it will limit us to get embrace the "Light."

It does matter how well we prepare our eternal soul in this lifetime.

Carl Jung, the famous co-developer of psychoanalytic theory, says that: "I simply believe that some part of the human self or soul is not subject to the laws of space and time." *Carl Jung, Mog, p.72*

Ultimately we must come to the realization that logic may not provide all the answers. The Universal Consciousness exists in an unseen dimension that I called the Divine Dimension, which like the soul is not physically connected to the human experience and yet it is very much a part of our being. And so, it could be said that the Universal Consciousness is resident in the realm of the soul. Is it then that we can find the answers to these questions in spiritual observance?

The answer is in the form of a question: is the heart the seat of the soul? We think with our brain and we feel with our heart. Where then is the mind? Is the mind the conscience of the soul? Our language is infused with references to the heart and its response to feelings of tenderness, sadness, happiness, emotion and state of mind. Instinct drives us to look at the heart as epitomizing heroism and altruism, while the brain drives us to logical and methodical actions. The heart doesn't think though. It must therefore be the mind where all brain activity is categorized and directed.

I think I said this before: the soul and the mind are pure energy and are linked in some way to the physical body. I believe that the soul is linked to the heart through one of the 4 universal forces and the mind is linked as an overlay to the brain. It is the electromagnetic force that is the glue that binds the mind and the soul to the body. Why are humans the only animals in the universe that possess a rational soul? It is because we are all participants in the universal consciousness, as evidenced by the common knowledge we share in the unfoldment of human destiny.

The brain processes information while the mind, attached to the soul, uses that information to mirror forth our personality. That is why some souls affect us, deeply, for the beauty shines bright with rays of hope and expectant jubilation. Others are dark with hopelessness, despair and malevolence.

Concepts are relational. When we view things within a certain perspective, this is often at the expense of its intended truth or implied truth. It causes us to view it with a tinge of expectancy, which is with our minds already made up with a conditioned answer formulated prior to understanding the essential verity and with the perception of it in an oblique way.

The personality of your being, its development, its advancement, its progression towards that which is sociably, ethically and humanly fashionable needs to be actively nurtured and developed in such a way that the brain is trained to make the neuron to neuron cell connections to put us into step with the rest of our kind. It is every person's responsibility to gather the knowledge for the advancement of our own eternal soul and all other souls as well, for the improvement of human destiny. It is a forward moving awareness through our presence here that forces us to unravel the mysteries of our existence. The more we can connect to the mysteries of this present existence the better we will be able to navigate the flow of life itself. So it is a multifunctional reality, our own development and the development of mankind as part of the human identity we all carry with us. To distance ourselves from the social responsibility, that is the knowledge and development from the common good is to detach ourselves from the reality of our very birth into this world and deny that we are all from the single source to develop the common tread in discovering that which binds us together. It is a continuous, never ending search that is based on further discovery of the human capacity while utilizing that which we have already uncovered. We do have control, to a certain extent over our own brain,

The development of the human brain anchored to a strong social connect is characteristic in Western society and thus humanity's irresistible progression towards a more perfect world. Continually seeking the discovery for truth and relevance allows us a glimpse into the future by developing capacity to see a humanity that improves as it advances, making mistakes along the way, but also bettering itself by learning from those mistakes. The miracle of human existence is in its capacity to evolve into a more perfect image of its former self. By this I mean that the being of today, informed as it is with the cumulative knowledge of us all, has the capacity for the betterment of the human lot. There are encumbrances that make us stray, such as the selfish aggrandizement for our own material gains, but in the end we must all realize that for each one of us it is about becoming better than the former self. To sum it all up: The information that is essential to attaining our goal to reach the "Eternal Light" (God or Heaven) or whatever you chose to call "hereafter", is the sum total knowledge from your lifetime of living, here on this earth, which was in part, shaped by all the information from the ever advancing society in which you lived.

RATIONAL THOUGHT

Rational and irrational thought, though at opposite ends, are part of the same emotion. Rationality is not part of your "logic processor", the brain. It is an element that resides in the mind. When the brain processes a thought, the "mind's eye" is simultaneously fed the same thought. It is in the mind, your personality, where this thought takes form, is processed and acted upon in the way that your life's experience directs it to. If your life is made up of negative experiences: a dominating, bullying sibling, a domineering parent, a lack of encouragement and endless put-downs about your abilities, then any conclusions, in your mind, will be tinged with negative feelings. Negativity is that bleak outlook that makes us impotent, creates inertia and unable to function. It bears no true resemblance to a reaction that is logical or reasoned, even though it could be. It is a knee-jerk reaction that is intensely yours. We wonder why at times our reactions are different from what some might term "normal" conditioned responses. The "normal" reactions are those programmed responses that are taught and learned, the social part of our psyche. The "normal" differs from person to person and culture to culture.

Conditioned responses are expected of us in our interaction with others. It is what makes us civil, social animals. Why do we react with anger at times when our brain processes someone's personal comment about us? We feel threatened by it. Our mind perceives that it diminishes us and reacts not in a logical sense, but rather in a passionate sense. Passion is good. We all need it. Passion is the "sauce piquant" of life and makes our minds not merely a sponge that soaks up life's offerings without response or reaction, but with excitement and vibrancy. It makes us all works of art in progress. The passion, however, needs to be tempered with the spice of moderation. We don't share our soul with anyone else. The independent search for knowledge and the maturing of the soul is an individual pursuit drawing on the resources in the universal subconscious and the conscious investigation of truth. Oddly enough, we do share the results of the individual pursuit for truth with the rest of humanity through this collective subconscious. The spirit is changeless, indestructible. The progress and development of the soul, the joy and sorrow of the soul are independent of the physical body.

If a friend, if a love causes us joy or pain prove true or false, it is the soul that is affected. If our dear ones are far from us, it is the soul that grieves, and the grief or trouble of the soul may react on the body.

When we find truth, constancy, fidelity, and love, we are happy; but if we meet with lying, faithlessness, and deceit, we are miserable.

These are all things pertaining to the soul, and are not bodily ills. Thus, it is apparent that the soul, even as the body, has its own individuality. But if the body undergoes a change, the spirit need not be touched. The same thing applies to the spirit of man. Though death destroys his body, it has no power over his spirit. This is eternal, everlasting, both birthless and deathless.

Throughout history, man has arrived at many different conclusions about how we came to be. He has hotly contested which of the two, evolutionism or creationism, is right. Advocates for the two theories have competed fiercely. Now it appears evident that the two are collaborating in order to understand our origins. "What is rational thought? Why must we be witness to the unfoldment of the universe? Why can't it just evolve without my witness to it? What can I do, even as I witness some of its intricacies? Without knowing why, it seems purposeless. We have no control over what happens, even if we know, right?

Rational thought is the ability to use logic to figure out something or the ability to reason and to acquire knowledge. Additionally, we have free will to choose our actions. These cycles of birth, death and decomposition are pre-ordained, we cannot control them, and we are part of the eternal loop.

Metaphysics implies: It is what it is and no further explanations can be had at this time in your existence. Nevertheless there are reasons why we have been given rational thought and one of them is that, for whatever reason, we must bear witness to the universe's unfoldment. Why that is, we don't know. All that we know is, that without man's witness, there is no knowledge, there is only existence… In the universe this Force that is in control of all things is just like the leader of the greatest orchestra in creation, and directs the symphony of life and death. It is surely a grand old tune. The soul that you were given needs knowledge. You think you know why. You will know, for sure, the reason why, after you pass from this existence into the next. The best example of comparing this life to the next is the baby in the womb and this present life. The baby is growing all its appendages, arms, legs, a nose, eyes to see with and it has absolutely no use for these in the womb. But the reason these are needed becomes abundantly clear when it is born into this life."

Just like today we think that God exists but we don't know for sure, the only way that we'll know for sure is in the next existence if we have developed spiritual eyes with which to see Him and that means that we must gain sufficient knowledge to be able to be in His presence and not be blinded by the Light. That is our mission in this life. We need to be a lot smarter on a spiritual level than we are now otherwise we won't be able to perceive him but in a state of "ignorance."

Whether or not you believe in God, you must admit, that there is something Greater than us at work in our earthly existence and that it seems to control the order of things. So, if we agree, we'll call it, for the lack of a better definition, the "God" universe. And even though it is all around us and within us, it manifests itself as pure energy. Unknowable to us, other than that we know that it has to do with the expansion of a super dense energy source. This source exploded, for lack of a better word, into a myriad of sub component parts of matter and energy. We, of course, form an integral part of this cosmic soup. Not understanding the whole because of the parts is a plight that we've been attempting to resolve in order to gain an understanding of why it is that we have been created in this way. This little bit of energy that we call our own is given to us with the objective that we must somehow alter that bit of energy, make it better, so to speak, impart it with knowledge so that it can eventually, armed with this wisdom become part of an entity we assume exists but of which we know very little. This is the theory of the very large, distinct and separate, but never the less the most confounding thing that insistently grabs centre stage in our consciousness. Albert Einstein et al did much of their life's research by developing theories that attempt to explain. We've always struggled with the concept of defining what or who God is. The inevitable answer we arrive at is that God is unknowable. In the world of energy there is no time, just energy. There is no logic at work here and there is no fast forward or reverse, night or day, no seasons, no good or bad, just energy. We can't explain it; all we can do is think it. That's all we really know, and if God wills it, is that through whatever means He does it lets certain people, we call them, Messengers or Prophets of God, people that He appoints and instills them with the very qualities that might describe His attributes. These become visible to us and we are then supposed to emulate them in order to educate our soul and educate the rest of mankind. That then is the mission of every soul that is born into this existence, this way station. Without this stop in our everlasting existence we become incapable to participate in the next stage of existence that is the merging of all souls with God. It is at once a never-ending process and one that improves the quality and quantity of the knowledge each soul yields to this common Energy.

EXPLANATION OF THE THEORY OF EVERYTHING

*T*o see *a world in a grain of sand…*
  William Blake, a poet, wrote the *Auguries of Innocence* some time in 1763.

> *"To see a world in a grain of sand, And a heaven in a wild flower, Hold infinity in the palm of your hand, And eternity in an hour.."*

If you listen carefully, you can hear God's voice telling us the story of the birth of the universe. It has no degrees of separation. Can you sense the sameness in all things from this poem? Everything in God's world of creation, including us, conforms to all of God's rules about birth, life and the hereafter. We're all related and we're all an integral part of the greater whole. We are all connected and whatever it is that we get at conception, we become responsible for it's education. We are therefore subservient, like everything else, to God's laws and the rules of integration and disintegration."

Integration consists of the bonding of different elements that occurs through what many believe to be a Divine Will and others believe it to be an act of circumstance. These compound elements so constructed form a strong bond that results in the "birth" of complex life forms. Disintegration is the reverse procedure of that process and results in the "death" and decomposition of that complex organism.

THE CHANGELESS FACE OF GOD

My ideas about life and truth are rooted in the belief that the order in the universe and therewith social order is pretty much pre-ordained by God and therefore we should give ourselves over to the idea that what we need to do is look after one another. Enlightenment or the age of reason, as it was often called, was popular in the time of William Blake, Isaac Newton and John Locke; all were a part of the new-enlightened thinking. They were also champions for this new age, but unlike Blake's views, Newton's laws cast the world in terms of natural laws beyond any spiritual force. John Locke held that people had the right to challenge a government that did not protect the natural rights of life, liberty and property. Blake's commentary treats life through the lens of spirituality and demonstrates that there are spiritual solutions to political problems. At the same time of heightened awareness, people were starting to question the existence of a God who had the power to send man into hell if He so wished and empower a tyrant for a king. These ideas would change the face of Europe forever. My views on enlightenment, as it relates to explaining everything, are relevant because it relates everything to a process that is governed by a super entity. Existence is organic and it mutates to the exigencies of the moment. What remains changeless is the face of God. The mystery lies in trying to comprehend the union of simple elements into complex structures. So what we need to do in life is attempt to understand the complexity that explains this process. There is, first of all, a process of attraction. This attraction is the same for all elements but is identified by many different words that describe its special ability, such as life, love, unity... and so on. For example, the attraction between two beings is demonstrated in their love for one another. This then causes these beings to come together and couple. The union then produces offspring furthering the ageless process. Adaptability is a term that explains that things evolve based on the needs of the time. Words can explain the universality of the wonder of all existence, but not in an efficient way and understanding lies not in the ability to deconstruct the words into simpler meanings, but it is attempting to understand the complexity of the word in its entirety. Just like the word "love" loses its meaning if you deconstruct it into simpler parts, because the

complexity of the word is what love means. So it is with
all existence; the single word, just like the single oak
seed has no real meaning until its grown into the mighty
oak tree, The single human cell cannot be seen in its
miraculous entirety until it is born, even though, even
as a single cell, it is a complete accurate representation
of its ultimate form, right down to the minutest details.
This is the special wonder of creation: We're all destined
to do what we are meant to do: In the vegetable kingdom
this means growing into what the vegetable is meant
to become; a squash seed becomes a squash plant that
grows squash, an apple seed becomes an apple tree...
Then we have the animal kingdom where the lower animals, in addition to the capacity of growing, also possess the capacity to act: A lion is hungry and his primal
impulse compels him to kill another animal in order to
survive. It's built into its DNA and it does so instinctively.
In the case of the higher animal, the human being, it has
all the same capacities, growth, instinctive and intuitive
thinking, and more importantly, the very quality that
sets us apart form the lower animals, rational thought
and free will.

SPIRITUALITY IS GOOD HEALTH IN ACTION

Through research and observation we are realizing that belief in a God, Faith and prayer will improve good health. Consequently, it can be said that those people who observe religious traditions have a lower risk of dying than those who don't. Belief in a loving, caring God yields a more favourable prognosis than those people who embrace a punitive, vindictive God. So it is, even though it can't be explained that people with a strong belief in a Greater Entity have a greater chance to survive deadly diseases and fare better than people who don't. Although the findings seem to be anecdotal, even the medical profession has witnessed many events of so called "miraculous" healing that remain unexplained. Not only is spirituality crucial to improve wellbeing there are other disciplines like Reiki, massage, Shiatsu,

Reconnective healing, Ayurvedic medicine, Shamanism and a whole host of others, yielding unexplained positive results in the treatment of disease. Why do we think we should not enlist the help of those disciplines, which have shown positive results to help us combat disease? Skeptics will maintain that there is nothing remarkable about people who get better suddenly, even after witnessing the practitioners of these non-medical disciplines at work. In the face of evidence that even doctors can't explain we would do well to not so easily discount these phenomena. The human brain is undeniably spiritually wired also and much goes on in the brain for which there is no scientific explanation. Just like we can influence our wellbeing in a negative way by thinking negative thoughts: "I feel lousy, sick, tired, in pain, ready to give up..." it is equally true that we can improve our wellbeing with positive thoughts: "I feel good today, ready to put my trust in the Almighty to heal me..." So why should we not entertain good thoughts instead of bad ones? Says Dr. Andrew Newberg, professor of radiology and psychology and religious studies at the University of Pennsylvania: "The way the brain works is so compatible with religion and spirituality that we're going to be enmeshed in both for a long time." *Gerard's Opus 22, the Joys of Health, Fitness & Youth Yours, in 22 Days, Gerard Dickert Schainuck, p. 122*

WHAT WE THINK IS OUR REALITY

Feelings of wellness can be easily tracked in the brain and so can prayer and meditation. When these functions occur in the brain it engages the frontal lobes, controlling personality, behaviour, emotions, judgment, planning, problem solving, speech, motor functions, intelligence, concentration and self awareness. The parietal lobes, at the back of the brain control prayer and meditation, sensory and visual information, language and mathematics, and causing the brain to quiet itself. The occipital lobe interprets vision, colour light and movement. The temporal lobe interprets language through an area called Wernicke's area and also houses the memory, hearing, organization and sequencing function. We create our own reality. Not just partially but in its entirety. To do this you use all parts of your brain incorporating your thoughts, vision, prayer, mediation, hearing, language, your feelings and your beliefs. You are completely in control and we are told that, as incongruous as it sounds, that even before birth you generate every event right down to the minutest detail. You start out with some pre-sets you can't change: whom your parents are, where you're born, your ethnicity or some inherited genetic pre-disposition. But on the highway of life you chose to travel on one of the million of lanes that are available. You chose your direction with your thoughts. These thoughts are based on powerful beliefs and guide you unerringly, whether right or wrong. Thus when something bad happens we're rarely willing to accept the blame for the bad choices we've made but we think that is what life did to us. Yet, cumulatively, we are all part of the great adventure called consciousness and once we've realized our responsibility we can start becoming masters over our life's experiences and no longer feel that we are victims of life. One of the first things we need to realize is that physical events almost never move our lives along and that in reality the opposite is usually true; events are formed in our minds and therefore what we imagine is what we experience. So as we stated before is that our own mind is responsible for our individual experiences and our common consciousness is the sum total of all our experiences. Every event, whether it is of the body, your mind or your spirit, is your own creation.

AN ENERGY THAT PRECEDES OUR EXISTENCE

All existence is begotten through energy and this energy in its myriad of frequencies comes from one single source and even though we cannot define it, this single source is central to all existence and it contains all the knowledge, no matter what its form, in the entire universe(s). The miracle of the "birth" of cells is that they come into existence replete with all knowledge, both known and unknown. So no matter how infinitesimal its own size it is fully formed with the ability to look after its own survival. The essence of human life is its complexity and the miracle of the birth of the human existence is through the formation of two cells that come into being "all knowing" to tend to the need of their own survival throughout the entire journey. These 2 cells combine and become a zygote and start replicating forever, each one, without exception, a perfect replica of the original 2; trillions of perfect replicas of the original until we are beautiful human beings. That is not the end of the journey: throughout their existence if any of the cells come under attack, all of its mates immediately spring into action and come to the aid of the cell under attack. The questions we must ask ourselves, if this assistance happens immediately how does it occur instantaneously and who is the "keeper" of that knowledge prior to the birth of the cells. How is this assistance communicated to the other cells? How are our cells given that knowledge, is it knowledge; if not what is it then? The closest I can define it is that it is "essence", a non-definable qualia that we know is present but not discernible, except through its abilities once the cells have it. So now we have three issues:

1. What is it?
2. What do we call it?
3. Where does it go when we no longer possess it?

We can call knowledge, consciousness and its quality is that we are conscious. It is two versions of the same thing. The third question is once we die where does the consciousness go? Since this knowledge is the same for all entities that come about, we cannot say that it comes about by chance, or chaos. So this means that there is some underlying force that is the keeper of it. Because all existence possesses the identical knowledge, the universal defense is unified to protect the whole. It makes sense that we learn from our cells and that we are involved in the survival of the whole, whether we know it or not. We have not yet arrived at the full spectrum of this knowledge. Firstly the cells communicate with each other via genetically encoded messages. Indirectly we take part in that conversation, whether we know it or not. How do we communicate? Through the positive and negative lifestyles we lead: A high fat diet, excessive drinking, poor sleeping habits, a stressful life, are all ways that you communicate messages to your cells, through your genes. Through other forms of communication, music, the arts, exercise, writing, poetry, any expression of beauty, prayer, excessive behaviour, addiction to substances. These are challenges to your genes to come to the aid, despite your own behaviour to combat the onslaught. Your cells have been encoded since you were only a zygote, with all they need to know. This knowledge is the sum total of all the "up to date" knowledge to keep them out of harms way. Even after all that, your cells know you can manage, through your life style, your body's wellness, good or bad. Some examples of communication:

1. Prayer is communicating with your body's cells through the universal life force
2. Meditation is communication directly with your body's cells
3. Ohm sound communication with your body through sound waves
4. Mathematics

5. Poetry
6. Prose
7. Exercise
8. Acting
9. Yoga
10. Massage
11. Reiki,
12. Reconnective healing
13. Arts
14. Singing...

WHAT DO WE CALL A SHARED UNIVERSE?

We all share the Universe and each of us is clamoring for their little corner of it by writing our own story, we should question what the meaning is of this collective experience. All of it occurs in real time and concurrently. Are we the main character in our story? We may very well be the main character with others playing a major role in our story. We know that we cannot all be the main character and even though each story plays out with the main character being the writer we must question whether something else is going on in the Universe. One thing we've come to know is that the universe of energy, particles and waves may very well be an infinite number of different universes all somehow interacting with each other. Whether as the future, the past or the present, they do differ one from the other. This kind of pronouncement is now popular since Stephen Hawking, shortly before his death, embraced the idea of the Multiverse, countless universes operating independent from one another and yet having interaction with each other. Shared experiences, unique experiences yet somehow interrelated makes the story of existence even more complicated than we imagined. It was assumed that all of us, including plants and other animals share particles with each other, is that still so in the Multiverse? It could be that as free particles floating around that we are enabled to use particles from any Universe, within the Multiverse. Although it does not seem likely that we can jump to different universes from our own, it does seem possible that we share things from other universes in what may be termed a no-mans land. All of the planet's evolutionary existence is contained within one single strand of DNA about 3 metres in length. Since the 1950's it is a well-known fact that DNA is the codification of life and that genes are susceptible to changes based on our own experiences, lifestyle and habits. For better or worse we are, individually, in control of our own genes, their wellness as well as their deterioration. What is important in this life is the individual contribution to the overall improvement of the human lot by contributing acquired knowledge and sharing it with all other existence. In the existence beyond, laden with the cumulative contributions of knowledge, as a whole, facilitates a smooth passage into the next existence. In that existence we are no longer separate universes but integral parts of the one Heavenly Universe, the unerring destination point for all beings. We wind up there replete with all that we've learned "here" yielding all to the Essence who sent us on our mission in the first place.

We are related to one another as human beings not so much through the human genome but more expressly through the primacy of life at the cell level and all of universal life is connected through cells. Since the one gene, one protein idea was fundamental to our thinking prior to the great human genome project, it was profoundly disappointing when we discovered, after the completion of the project and with the help of thousands of scientists worldwide, that of 120,000 genes that were analyzed, we found that the entire human genome consisted of fewer than 25,000 genes (*Source; the Biology of Belief, Bruce H. Lipton page 32)*, and those that make up who we, are the same as the ones that make up a banana or a monkey. So when we view life in all its glory we find that we have more in common with all of life in the Multiverse than merely life to each other through maternal and paternal human cells. The rules that govern all life are the same for all life and the results of the human genome project cause us to reflect on our ideas of genetic relationships with all other organisms. It no longer suffices to think that since we can communicate our knowledge to all other species we are at the top of the evolutionary scale.

So the common elements we share with all other life forms, at the gene level, are also those that draw us together more than set us apart from those other life forms. It is true, however, that since humans are mentally further advanced on the evolution scale we are at the very centre of discovery and the ones that can make sense of existence for all life forms and our responsibility, therefore, is not only to learn all we can but also to share it with all other organisms. If we don't have more functioning genes than most other life forms, what is it then that gives us our tremendous complexity and the ability to produce the conscious thoughts that set us apart from the rest of all other living organisms? In our mad dash to find the Holy Grail of human destiny in the genome, the scientific community should have come to the realization that genes were not controlling life. It is our destiny in life to gather the knowledge and share it with all other organisms to whatever extent that is possible, for without our witness to knowledge and our telling of it there is no knowledge. (The tree falling in the forest without our witness, does it make a sound? is a good example of the importance of information sharing.)

THE PARADOX OF EXISTENCE

I t is paradoxical that we try to find proof and unravel the mysteries of metaphysical existence without having access to the necessary connection points. From a purely dimensional perspective, we know but four of the many more that would lead us to meaningful discovery of the intricacies of the universe(s), those that are beyond the realm of this earthly existence. Time and space are the two dimensions that will offer up a treasure trove of discoveries. As has already been demonstrated: time beyond this earthly existence does not exist; at least not in the restrictive format that we perceive here. Hence the paradox to attempt to unravel the mysteries of life beyond, while we are still here, when upon the passing from this life the entire mystery will automatically reveal itself in all its' glory; at least we expect it will. So with the removal of the time constraint we will be able to peer into the universe, unencumbered. We will come to know all that is unknown to us, in the next stage of our existence. At least we will discern all knowledge but if we did not learn and understand it here it may not make much sense to us there and it won't be a pleasant sensation. It is our mission while we are alive in this bodily frame to gather up as much knowledge as possible so that in the next stage all that we've learned here will make sense there (wherever there is) such as:

1. The existence of a greater entity than we are
2. The beginning and the end of things
3. The exact value of infinity
4. The understanding of non locality
5. The answer to the uncertainty principle
6. Unlimited number of universes

Man's spirituality has become veiled and in its stead we are now afflicted with a voracious material appetite. Its appeal is relentless because we have become conditioned to impulses that are at once all consuming and selfish. The vitality of man's belief in God is on life support and nothing but the total collapse of the present socio-economic system, that has laid hold on us, can impel mankind back to spiritual consciousness. What else but the essence of God's potent revelation can cleanse man's suffering soul and nurse it back to wholesome wellness. As difficult and confounding as this may seem, the great challenge of changing our baser instincts into heavenly power is one that man has been empowered to accomplish, particularly in this time, when humanity has attained its collective maturity. God's Words are endowed with such power that they alone have the capacity to provide the healing balm for man's recovery. God has set this time aside for man to turn to Him for Counsel and if we choose to ignore it, serious suffering will assail us from all directions. The glorious heights man can in this day attain are as yet unrevealed. The time is fast approaching when the possibilities of so great a favour will, by virtue of God's Promise to mankind, be revealed. Since God's reality is an ever-progressing revelation, mortal man has now become enabled to uncover the limitless potentialities of God's latest Covenant, that is at once the Greatest fulfillment of all of Gods previous Promises and will at the same time propel mankind into the "Most Great Peace" lasting for one thousand years. Even though the forces of all the nations are arrayed against Him, the tide of God's irresistible decree cannot be stopped. We have been created to carry forward this ever-advancing civilization and the virtues that accompany it are dignity and justice, compassion, mercy and loving-kindness. God, in His infinite wisdom, invites us to drink our fill from the stream that flows through His Heavenly Grace, while at the same time, recognizing the reason for which we were created. The human race is as one soul and one body and each one of us is poised to win our share of God's good grace and mercy. Today is the day that eclipses all other days; how great is the happiness that awaits us when we decide to forsake all the things of this material world, with the express desire to receive all of God's blessings in its staid. Let's all rejoice, for this is the time that the long awaited has unlocked the gate to man's heart to receive all His bounties and to proclaim the Glad tidings of God's nearness. His clarion call has lifted the veil that obscures man's vision. It is time to arise and muster the strength to strive to attain God's favour. Let's bestir ourselves so that the ephemeral time of our lives may not be lost on wasteful pursuits. Our days on this earth are numbered and as our bodies are laid to rest, the everlasting souls will soar with the culmination of our performances to face our Maker and it is then that each of us will recognize whether, that which we accomplished on this earth, was sufficient to gaze upon the beauty of God.

MAN'S EXCELLENCE AND DIGNITY

The evidences of God's perfection is enshrined in every atom and but for the potency of that perfection not one living being could exist. Man, in particular, has been selected as the recipient for all of God's attributes to such an extent that no other created living thing in the universe can surpass him. God says: "Man is my mouthpiece, and I am his mystery." This is repeatedly evidenced in all of God's scriptures:" We will surely show them Our signs in the world and within themselves." And then He says: "And also in your own selves: will ye not, then, behold the signs of God?" And yet again: "be ye not like those who forget God, and whom He hath therefore caused to forget their own selves. He hath known God who hath known himself." *Baha-u-llah, Bahá'í World Faith –*

Man is God's noblest being. He is greater than all other created things and is the perfect rendition of God's expression. God cautions that now is not the time to rest on the fleeting things of this material world, but to arise and teach the Cause of God. Let's all of us teach God's Cause and be loving to one another. In this day God has enkindled the world with His Fire and He bemoans those that fail to be afire with His flame. His main concern is to help the ones who are estranged. Our attitude towards our fellow man must be so strong that it clearly shows forth God's most excellent qualities. Those souls who are in Heaven understand this much better those living beings residing on this earth. Let us hope that the Almighty grant that your desires and unrestrained passions will not keep you from that which God has ordained for you.

ACTIONS OF THE RIGHTEOUS

We must be generous and share our wealth, and be patient in adversity. Trust your neighbour and earn your neighbour's trust. Help the poor, counsel the wealthy and be a healing balm to the needy. Temper your judgment and speak no evil. Be fair to all men and be humble. Be a shining beacon and a safe harbor for the stranger. Defend those who are oppressed. Let your acts be righteous. Be a home for the stranger, a balm to the suffering and strength to the fleeing. Offer guidance to the sightless and wise counsel to the wayward. Be truthful, virtuous and just. Do not be petty and do not be a mischief-maker. Don't be heedless and always devote yourself to the betterment of humanity.

WHY WERE WE CREATED?

We were created to carry forward an ever-advancing civilization. In this day all the books of God have been unsealed. It is not up to us to decide the time for the revelation of His Healing Message, but to be a part in the revelation of His Glad Tidings. Ascertain for yourself whether or not you are such a light and be happy for what God has decided for you in this day. Let justice be your guide and do not transgress the limits of moderation. Ponder God's words and be not of those who are in doubt.

CAN WE MANUFACTURE LIFE BY CHANGING DNA?

DNA is deoxyribonucleic acid, a material that is able to self-replicate itself in all living organism and is the main constituent of chromosomes. It is also the carrier of genetic information. Life is fashioned around the information in DNA. This is really profound and just as the English language is made up of twenty-six letters of the alphabet. When combined into words, allow me to tell you the story I'm going to tell you today, DNA is made up of genetic letters that, when combined into genes, allow cells to produce proteins, strings of amino acids that fold up into complex structures that perform the functions that allow a cell to do what it does, to tell its stories. The English alphabet has 26 letters, and the genetic alphabet has four. They're pretty famous. Maybe you've heard of them. They are often just referred to as

G, C, A and T. But it's remarkable that all the diversity of life is the result of four genetic letters. Imagine what it would be like if the English alphabet had four letters. What sort of stories would you be able to tell? What if the genetic alphabet had more letters? Would life with more letters be able to tell different stories, maybe even more interesting ones?

CAN WE MAKE BETTER CHOICES?

B ased on the choices we make, our life can develop much different from its present evolvement. We are creatures of habit who are shaped by past experiences. Does that mean that we can't change the choices we make?

Nobel Prize winning physicists have proven beyond doubt that the physical world is one large sea of energy that flashes into and out of being in milliseconds, over and over again.

NOTHING IS SOLID

This is the world of Quantum Physics. It has been proven that thoughts are what fashions and holds together this ever-changing energy field into 'objects' that we perceive. So why do we see a person instead of flashing energy clusters? Imagine life evolving like a movie reel. A movie is a collection of sequences of about 24 frames a second. Each frame is separated by a gap. However, because of the speed at which one frame replaces another, our eyes get cheated into thinking that we see a continuous and moving picture. Think of television. A TV tube is simply a tube with heaps of electrons hitting the screen in a certain way, creating the illusion of form and motion. This is what all objects are anyway. You have 5 physical senses (sight, sound, touch, smell, and taste). Each of these senses has a specific spectrum (for example, a dog hears a different range of sound than you do; a snake sees a different spectrum of light than you do; and so on). In other words, your set of senses perceives the sea of energy from a certain limited standpoint and makes up an image from that.

It is not complete, nor is it accurate. It is just an interpretation.

All of our interpretations are solely based on the 'internal map' of reality that we have created for ourselves, and thus a perceived reality. Our 'map' is made up of our personal life's collective experiences and is unique to us. This invisible energy determines what the energy forms. So ultimately our thoughts literally move our personal universe along on a particle-by-particle basis to create our physical adventure. When we look around we notice that our physical world starts as an idea that grows as it becomes entwined with others, until it has expanded into a full fledged adventure with a plot and a story line and you literally become the main actor in your story of life.

Your life becomes what you have imagined and believed in most.

Your world is literally your mirror of life, enabling you to experience, in the physical plane what you imagine as your truth ... until you decide to change it. Quantum physics shows us that the world is not the hard and unchangeable thing it may appear to be. Instead, it is a very fluid place continuously built up using our individual and collective thoughts. What we think is true is really an illusion, almost like a magic trick. Fortunately we have begun to uncover the illusion and most importantly, how to change it.

WHAT IS THE BODY MADE OF?

The human body consists of nine integral systems, including Skeletal, Muscular, Reproductive, Digestive, Circulatory, Respiratory, Nervous, Urinary and Endocrine. And those in turn are made up of tissues and organs. And tissues and organs are made up of cells. And cells are made up of molecules and these in turn make up atoms. The atoms are made up of sub-atomic particles. And finally subatomic particles are made of pure energy.

We are pure energy-light in its most beautiful and intelligent configuration. Energy that is constantly changing beneath the surface and we can control it all with a most powerful mind. You and I are big stellar and powerful Human Beings. If you could see yourself under a powerful electron microscope and conduct other experiments on yourself, you would see that you are made up of clusters of ever-changing energy in the form of electrons, neutrons, photons and so on and so is everything else around you. Quantum physics tells us that it is the act of observing an object that causes it to be there wherever and however we observe it. It is important to recognize that an object does not exist independent of its observer! So, as you can see, your observation, your attention to something, and your intention, creates that thing. This is scientific and proven. Your world is made of spirit, mind and body. Each of those three, spirit, mind and body, has a function that is unique to it and not shared with others. What you see with your eyes and experience with your body is the physical world. The body is an effect, created by a cause. This cause is a thought. The body cannot create itself. It can only experience and be experienced … that is its sole function. Thought cannot experience. It can make up things, interpret them and draw conclusions. It needs a contingent world to experience itself. Finally, spirituality is the essence of all that is. It gives purpose and meaning to life and can and does exist on a different plane and we can draw upon it to give profound meaning to our life. Naturally spirituality has different meanings, each depends on the level of interaction we can muster with the rest of the world around us. When we see ourselves as spiritual entities we signal three things. The first thing is that we view the world of existence not merely as a way station but a world requiring interaction with others. It seems that today spirituality without religion is gaining popularity. Second, it is believed that many of the self-reflective disciplines such as yoga, meditation and others embrace spirituality as a required by-product. Third, spirituality enforces a set of human values that encompasses righteousness, honesty, love and selfless service to humanity as a way to showcase our understanding of altruism and the application of kindly acts towards others without expecting these acts to give us entry into heaven. Being a source of good to all of mankind is sufficient reward in itself. It just makes us feel good. So, the fulfillment of our mission on earth is the applied use of our God-acquired talents.

It means that we must seek with spiritual eyes because we must not only learn the attributes of God, but we must also apply them for the good of humanity. Within this context, we can actually understand the meaning of life and education of the soul, and we only have this one lifetime to work on educating our soul. We have no time to waste, for if we live this existence without having fulfilled our mission, it will have consequences in the next life. By the way, everything that comes into existence has a purpose. Our purpose in this life is to know God. Our mission in life is to serve God and this servitude is only visible by how we serve our fellow human beings. What if you don't believe there is a God? What happens to the soul then? To the best of our ability, our words describe a vast range of things. Sometimes not very well, but we try the best we can to use words to communicate complex ideas that often defy mere words. Sometimes we use words to attempt to describe events, social phenomena, or people and entities. Using the word 'God' for example, an imaginary entity is one such word. It does not describe a human being, but rather an entity that is beyond our comprehension and defies any other description. As you well know, there are other such words that are used to describe the same entity, such as 'The Primal Point,' 'The Creator,' 'The Light,' 'The Primal Source,' 'Point of Adoration,' 'Yahweh,' etc. It seems that we have done that to facilitate a more common understanding of the word 'God.' He has become popularized in history, in re-occurring Biblical events and in His perfection. His essence may not be knowable to anyone, but His attributes are mirrored perfectly by the privileged few He has appointed as His mouthpiece. That is how we perceive Him, not as a knowable essence, but as a metaphysical truth most of us embrace because we need to take guidance from a more perfect life for the perfecting of our soul. Most importantly, however if we do not want to name that essence that we know exists as God and because the entanglement we have with it we've got to name it something. That something cannot be 'nothing' because if there is nothing, then non-locality and entanglement, two crucial aspects of quantum physics, cannot exist. So no matter what we want to believe, God or no God, we must obtain the capacity here, in this life, to recognize that essence, since it will be an integral part of what we will become.

Those that do not believe in another existence past this bodily one, dismiss the importance to prepare for anything else but final death and nothing else. Well let me say this about that: We are contradicting two important laws of thermodynamics.

The first law of thermodynamics: Energy is constant and can change from one state to another state, but that energy can neither be created nor destroyed.

The second law of thermodynamics: The second law applies to entropy. Very simply, energy—like heat for example—always flows from hot to cold and never from cold to hot. There comes a point in this energy flow when all the energy is of the same temperature, when there is no more energy flow and the energy has reached equilibrium; in other words, no more heat is produced when it reaches this state. That is the law of entropy: the energy still exists, but it has changed its state from usable to unusable.

When we are alive the body is alive and the body is full of energy. Thus when we die, the body dies but the energy, based on the 1st law of thermodynamics does not disappear. Based on the 2nd law of thermodynamics the energy is in an equilibrium condition (here but not usable). Where does the energy go? It is during the time of altering states, from life to death to another state, that the energy resets itself so that it can again be used on its next adventure.

Everything in the universe or universes is made up of energy. Our bodily frames, automobiles, trees in the forests, houses, your favorite food, everything that you observe as solid matter is ultimately but vibrating atoms, in other words, energy. So too, are all forms of sentiment. Energy is discernible in vibrating wave patterns and any event that occurs or any action we undertake within the energy matrix leaves its own pattern or footprint. Luckily for us, energy is slowed down enough in this life so that it is observable and we can actually experience the consequences of our actions. Everything we do as individuals, such as walking, sleeping, thinking about the hockey game, hoping that Canada will win an Olympic gold medal, in short everything we do interacts with other activities within the energy grid and has consequences for all that are involved in the billions of activities that occur concurrently at all times. Many clash with each other. We do all interact with energy, sometimes in ways that are detrimental to us and to universal harmony. It is during those periods that we grow better or worse physically, mentally or spiritually. There is a confluence of occurrences that affect us in positive or negative ways. We speak of the fourth dimension as the space/time continuum, but I think it should be the space/time/energy continuum. We can interact in positive ways within the dimension, causing good positive things to happen or conversely we can interact in a negative or malevolent way, thereby eliciting dark energy (dark, as in 'not good') to emerge. The choice is always ours. The distinct vibrations caused by our interaction with energy or the interruption of the universal energy flow—resulting in the various experiences of life—aid in fashioning our destiny. These interactions can cause us to be in disharmony within the energy continuum and thus, ultimately we need to be reconnected to it. These disconnected occurrences establish distinct life patterns that make us all unique and different. We use what we've learned to interact within the energy grid in a way that sometimes helps us and at other times is not so good for us. Thus, we must optimize our connectedness to the entire energy spectrum, without really interrupting it. Sometimes these interruptions disconnect us and send us on tangents that can manifest themselves in disease or ill health and a general disconnect in our lives.

"One basic lesson you can take away from what I've told you is that everything is composed of energy. Don't ever forget that. Your harmony with this oneness of energy is your state of consciousness. Consciousness and the concept of our reality, yours and mine, is that consciousness is energy and that consciousness itself must therefore conforms to the same rules of gravitational pull as all other matter or energy. It is simply that gravity cannot be merely regarded as some kind of 'emergent phenomenon,' secondary to other physical effects, but that it is a 'fundamental component' of our physical reality. In other words it bends."

CONFLICTING THEORIES

"We are all conflicted by one theory that says that a God created our existence 'in His own image' and by an opposing theory that states that the universe came about by accident. Both tell a fascinating story. The first tells of the story of creation and a 'First Force' that created existence. The second talks about a theory of chaos. However, that is not a point I want to explore here. It doesn't matter whether or not you believe in an energy source that started existence—in what has been called the 'big bang,' or this Primal Force, which then split this tremendous energy source into four separate forces: gravity, electromagnetic energy, the weak nuclear force and the strong nuclear force. Science and religion come together in explaining that on this point there is consensus in understanding the significance that everything sprang from a primal force. In religion, we call it

God and in science we call it the unified field or string theory. Scientists have also come to agree on a handful of principles that have fused a theory of exquisite simplicity, called the 'standard model.'

"The standard model suggests that there exist only two classes of indivisible particles, called quarks and leptons. As it turns out, the right combination of quarks and leptons can make up any atom and therefore any type of matter in the universe. It is also significant that all matter is held together by any one of the four known forces I outlined earlier. It sounds pretty simple doesn't it? But hold on to your hat. Did I say indivisible particles? Scientists have long theorized that there are still smaller particles than quarks and leptons. We now know that by smashing these particles together they split. That is how we discovered the Higgs boson, also dubbed the 'God particle.' We can only wonder if even that is truly the smallest or if we will perhaps discover something smaller yet!

We also know from experience that gravity is something that holds us to this earth and if it were not present we would fall off the earth. But what gravity actually consists of is less well understood. All that I can say is this: the laws of attraction and repulsion do not apply in the universe the same way that they apply to our everyday existence in other words, to you and me. In the universe, attraction and repulsion work simultaneously. Structures are formed and destroyed at the same time. If you liken the universe to a bowl of thick soup, you can visualize everything in this thick soup, vegetables, pieces of meat, and everything else, floating together seemingly independent of each other; yet we can observe an underlying order; in other words, everything is connected: you and I, trees, planets, and so on. Of course, to make things more realistic, the other dimension that we need to be aware of, is that the soup, as it is in the universe, is not contained in a bowl. Also that in the universe, planets collide, stars explode and everything seems to be freely floating. There is no explanation for these phenomena. They just are. When the big bang occurred, everything that was previously one single point of enormous energy was split into component parts that, temporarily at least, showed forth an expanding view with different characteristics of the same thing. Now we're trying to find the unified theory that can explain everything. It lets us observe things in a solid state, when the expanded energy fused with others and became solid matter, while others remained pure energy, like gravity. It's incredible that science is now looking at a vastly expanding universe and trying to find the meaning of its origin. And the irony is that one of the forces, thermodynamics, governs the very thing that has no mass, the photon, one of the building blocks of the atom. And the universe, as we know it, is made up of empty space or to use another word 'nothing' and then there is something. Is it because the space is reserved? And yet all the component parts of the big bang seem to conform to the laws of attraction and repulsion.

The question still remains, why is it that things in the universe defy these laws of attraction and repulsion. Why do they push and pull at the same time? Is it that we perhaps don't know enough yet? Why do the stars not seem to abide by the laws of thermodynamics? We know that the electromagnetic force works with, and is, energy and the rules for this energy are pretty much defined in the laws that govern energy, that is, the laws of thermo-dynamics. We also know that everything is energy even though its state can be observed and made to behave as matter, such as light for example. Whatever its state, however, it affects us and interacts with our life at every moment of our existence. Just as this first event, the big bang, sprang from a primal point, a point of unimagina-ble density; it not only split the energy force into four, but it also spewed matter into a continually expanding uni-verse. Therefore, we conjecture that at one time, before the big bang, this was all condensed into one. To be both participant in and observer of this event is a testament to the importance of our role in this life. Ironically we are also the observation. Without our testimony, this event could not be witnessed and therefore did not 'happen.' Our consciousness is the only reality to anything that happens in the cosmos.

CONSCIOUSNESS IS OUR REALITY

Here is an example of how the idea came about that our testimony to events is reality. Let's suppose that you and someone you know do something together, for example, discover a cure for cancer. You both did it together and you're both well satisfied that you did the job well. But let's say that your partner, who was part of the process of invention and witnessed it, develops Alzheimer's disease and does not remember the event; in his mind, it never happened, but you witnessed and participated and you know for a fact that it did take place. Who is right and who is not? Now suppose that both of you have Alzheimer's and neither of you remembers what you did together. You did not write it down and the cure remains unrecorded. Was the cure discovered? And so it goes with everything. If we all develop Alzheimer's and we no longer recall all the events that formulated man's evolving maturation, then none of it took place, right? It simply never happened. Do you see what I am saying? That is why the role we play in this conscious state with all its knowledge-seeking and sharing is vital not only to our ever-evolving soul but to all created existence.

The next part of the puzzle is that the soul has a clear responsibility to fulfill its mission to gather knowledge, so that it will be able to progress to another level of existence when it leaves the body. How and when is the soul 'ready' to leave the body?"

MISSION COMPLETE

When the body dies the soul must leave the body, whether or not the soul has completed its mission or not. If the soul has not fully matured it can be likened to the baby growing in the mother's womb and being born without having grown its legs for example. That will make it very difficult for the newborn baby to get around unaided. So the baby in the womb has to fulfill its full cycle of growth before it can be born fully developed so that it can function perfectly in this life. It is the same for the soul. It needs to fulfill its destiny completely, in order to progress into its next existence. By using another analogy it will clarify the function of the soul: When we compare the body to a power station and the brain to a lamp and the soul to a powerful light bulb attached to a battery. The power station provides the lamp with its energy that in turn makes the bulb glow continuously, while at the same time it recharges the battery. Of course, without the power source, the lamp cannot function. The lamp, the bulb and the battery are unique to the body. When the body dies, the power station shuts off and no longer gives its energy. But the bulb, with its battery needs to find a new lamp to plug into. What happens next is that the bulb will now have to rely on a more universal power source, such as, for example, the energy from the sun. When the bulb with its charged storage battery (the soul) detaches from the lamp (your brain), it is a huge mass of energy, now in a state of equilibrium. The new journey that the bulb and its stored energy is embarking upon (your soul with its stored knowledge) will be made easier, based on what you've learned in your life and how you have applied what you learned. And the more you have learned the better, because within that experience is embedded the roadmap to your new energy source (God). If there are pieces of the roadmap missing, it will make the journey that much more arduous and unpleasant.

It's important to remember that light is energy, and that it can behave as a wave as well as a particle. Light bends because of gravity and this demonstrates that light has mass and is also a particle and the fact that your thoughts are observable, they can be seen as waves using a device known as an 'MRI', or magnetic resonance imaging machine, which can scan the brain in real time. These vibrating waves, of different frequencies, shorter waves for the higher frequencies and longer waves for the lower frequencies reflect the activity of your brain.

Not only are thoughts waves of energy, our unique ability to think in a very special way that is called rationality and as far as we know, we humans are the only species equipped with the capacity to reason. And so all these rational thoughts are believed by some, such as the psychiatrist Karl Jung to be contained in what he named the 'universal human subconscious.' The knowledge that is gathered by the rational soul becomes a part of the universal pool of knowledge. This knowledge is pooled with all the other knowledge from all other souls and that then represents the common pool of all the knowledge that Dr. Jung calls the 'universal subconscious.' This knowledge is passed on to all souls."

When a newborn dies at birth or shortly thereafter? A soul enters into this life *tabula rasa,* that is, like a blank slate without prior knowledge, except for what is termed as the 'universal subconscious.' Nothing about this life has yet been inscribed in its soul. The baby's soul is as pure as God's white light. If at any point during its early life the baby dies, it goes straight to 'heaven,' because nothing from this physical life has made any impression upon its soul. God has given babies and infants a free pass into heaven.

CAN WE FORCE OUR WILL UNTO MAN

As human beings we all possess a free will to do as we please. There is no way that we can force our will unto others, all that we can offer is the truth and then it is up to others to accept it or not. Unfortunately in the protraction of man's present blind state of materialism the consequences of making wrong choices results in a humanity that is distracted and completely unaware of the great suffering of a crying humanity. Most of us, if we so choose, have the capacity to fulfill a higher destiny, instead, we choose to sink to great depths of degradation and dwell with the meanest creatures. All of us should take a sabbatical from our present state of inertia and concentrate our efforts to learn about the present state of the world. We must realize that the entire purpose for our presence on earth is to learn and to improve the human lot until the world and we become the best that we can be and so fulfill our spiritual destiny. Each of us bears this great responsibility. Man's potential, the full measure of our destiny, the pent-up excellence that we possess must be used in the service of all humanity. That is the purpose to be in this life, on this earth, in this time. We need to appreciate the fact that destiny and free will are not mutually exclusive and if we think of our destiny there is an inherent direction that is relentless in its pursuit for the betterment of the world. But it is important to free ourselves from the superstitions of the past and become investigators of the true reality. We will then realize that God's Light shines to illuminate humanity's path of evolution. The unfoldment is gradual and progressive and never beyond our ability to comprehend. God's eternal law that deals with man's attainment of immortality remains immutable, unchangeable and eternal in all ages, but mundane laws governing human conduct that regulate observing the Sabbath, marriage, divorce, reward and punishment etc... vary from age to age to take into account the capacity of the people to comprehend. It is the loftiest station for man to fulfill his high destiny. Let him seize the opportunity to provide pure and goodly acts of kindness.

THE QUANTUM FIELD THEORY

The wave, particle conundrum
How can something be both a particle and a wave? The explanation is as counter intuitive as is its concept. Albert Einstein explained it as two contradictions of reality: separately we cannot understand the wonder of light; it is not a particle nor is it a wave because neither adequately explains the phenomenon on its own and also they are contradictory, but together they explain it perfectly. Niels Bohr, the famous Danish Nobel prize physicist, dubbed it a "duality paradox" and a metaphysical quirk of nature. It is a popularly held scientific theory that all waves are also particles and vice versa. The particle-wave duality functions well in physics while the impact of its meaning has not been thoroughly appreciated. Intuitively we feel that the theory is compatible and yet contradictory and we face the same dilemma when

we try to explain the harmony that must exist between science and religion. Science must provide logical proof that something is true, while religion is not bound by the same rules because God tells us something is true. It is a generally held belief that neither science nor religion can prove the other wrong, in other words: if religion tells us that something is right it cannot be proven wrong using scientific discourse and vice-versa. We must try to remember that what we think we observe as reality is not actual reality. All you see around you in your house, the furniture, paintings, dishes and cups, the furnace...do not appear to be moving and yet the atoms that make up these items are constantly in motion. We say that nothing moves because our eyes cannot see them move. Classical physics relies on physical observation to explain things to us and we're comfortable with that notion, whereas when we see the same things in quantum physics it cannot explain to our senses what is happening and even though the particles are actually moving we can't see it. We've learned in school that the earth is also in motion but we don't feel it. We've learned that the earth revolves around the sun at a speed of about 67,000 miles per hour. So although things do not appear to our senses to be true we've learned to accept them as true if someone can convince us. Talk to yourself in your head sounds different from talking out loud, to the outside world.

HOW DO WE SOUND?

Our own voices sound very differently inside our heads than they do to others. In fact, when people hear a sound recording of their voices for the first time, most don't like what they hear. It sounds strange and unfamiliar. Even so, that is how we sound to the outside world. Again, humans perceive one thing. Reality is another.

HOW DO WE SEE OURSELVES?

When we look in the mirror we see the reflection of who we are. Can we say, with a certainty, that this reflection is the 100% rendering of how others see us? Is this reflection exactly the same as if someone had taken our picture? Somehow I don't think that is how we look to the rest of the world. Also, since we typically see our self in the mirror everyday, the brain takes great liberty with what it sees. It presumes you look the same as before and only senses gross discernible differences. As with sound, we need to turn to the "outside" world to discover how we appear to others. And so it is that we imagine, because we cannot see through the eyes of others, what and how we look like.

General relativity and quantum mechanics are about as compatible as oil and water. Resolving differences between the theory of general relativity and the predictions of quantum physics remains a huge challenge, however, we are close to combine Einstein's General Theory of Relativity with quantum physics. The result could help provide a successful theory of quantum gravity. Caslav Brukner from the University of Vienna in Austria and Magdalena Zych from the University of Queensland have come up with a way to compare the way objects behave according to Einstein's theory with the behaviour as predicted by quantum theory. The behaviour of atoms and electrons, has demonstrated accurate results for forces at cosmic scales, while in the case of gravity the two theories have demonstrated wildly incompatible results. Einstein's theory revealed that gravity caused curves in space-time while another force, magnetism, in quantum theory was the result of fleeting particles between interacting objects. The question needs to be asked whether objects attracted by magnetic or electrical forces behave similarly when they are attracted by gravity from a nearby planet, for example? Physicists maintain that there is a close relationship between an objects' gravitational mass and its inertial mass. The principle is known as the Einstein's equivalence principle.

Professors Brukner and Zych proposed tests that would tease out the quantum behaviour from the gravitational acceleration by combining two principles to frame the problem. From Einstein's relativity they took the ubiquitous equation $E=MC^2$, that suggested that an object becomes heavier when it gains more energy. This even applies to an atom moving from a low energy level to a more excited state.

To this they added the principle of quantum super-position, which holds that particles can be smeared into more than one state at once. And since the different energy levels have different masses, then the total mass gets smeared across a range of values, too.

This prediction allowed the pair to propose tests that would tease out the quantum behaviour of acceleration. Another unit is the acceleration due to gravity. We can readily identify how gravity pulls at our own bodies and the objects around us and this lets us compare the speed of acceleration that surrounds us. We've heard the term g force used in space travel and it is the measure of acceleration but not force. We've also experienced g force, the force that pulls at our bodies, when we ride a roller-coaster and again to re-iterate, it is not the force but the speed of acceleration that creates the g force; it is what makes the ride so thrilling. The heavier the body the greater the g force. NASA, despite the immense power of the engine's rockets keeps acceleration under 3 g's, because a greater g force would put undue stress on the astronauts. Once the rocket is in orbit it goes into a free fall that simulates weightlessness. Humans can sustain g forces greater than 3 g's for short durations but sustained periods greater than 3 g's will ultimately cause blackouts. Zych was inspired to tackle the problem when thinking about a variant of Einstein's twin paradox. This arises as a consequence of relativity, and says that one twin travelling at high speed will age more slowly than the other, who remains stationary.

RESOLVING THE QUANTUM ENTANGLEMENT

The concept of non-locality
Quantum entanglement refers to the concept that every particle in the universe has a twin. The greatest minds in history and in particular Einstein could not get his head around the concept of non-locality. His view differed from that of his contemporary, Rabindranath Tagore, the world famous Indian writer and poet, with whom he had a running argument. They had their now faithful meeting at Caltech in 1930. It is not quite clear why Tagore would debate Einstein on such a scientific concept. Anyways, non-locality is of importance in understanding consciousness, being and reality. It's important to be able to understand that everything is related to everything else in the cosmos. Non-locality or non-local reality is one of those great mysteries in

quantum mechanics that has a great impact on our existence. Even though it has confounded some of the greatest minds, scientist John Bell, a Scottish physicist in what is now known as Bell's theorem, proved its existence. His argument in 1964, on a leave from CERN when he attended a year at Stanford University, went like this: Every particle has a twin, even if these particles are separated by millions of light years. Here's a simple analogy: if I tell a particle here a funny story, then its twin, that is found a million light years away will laugh at my funny story. Not only does it transcend distances but it happens instantaneously, as if there were no separation between these particles at all. Einstein, during his now-famous meetings with Tagore at Caltech in 1930, called it spooky science and maintained that it violated the rules of cause and effect. First, he said it went counter to Newton's Laws of motion, particularly Newton's third law: For every action there is an opposite and equal reaction. It also defied Einstein's rule, which held that nothing could travel faster than the speed of light. So no matter how fast the interaction was, the interaction between the particles could never be instantaneous. Tagore claimed that it did neither, since the interaction between the twin particles transcend the time-space principle and was therefore not bound by the rules of causality or the speed of light restriction. We now know that Einstein was proven wrong and that Tagore was right. Why didn't Einstein get it right away? The answer to Einstein was that the argument was counter-intuitive and that there must exist a harmony between all science and religion. It is nevertheless important that we appreciate the interconnectedness between particles. The fact is that everyone's existence is conjoined with that of every other being, and this means that at one time or another: we've shared most of all our particles with everything else in the cosmos. The particles that make up our unique being have been continually shared by everything else in the cosmos. Some scientists say that our body and its parts are renewed approximately every year; that is, you grow a new spine, blood vessels, heart, lungs, skin, etc. annually! Thus, we're not so different one from another. The genes we think are unique to us are not so unique after all, as we share 58% of the same genes with a banana and some 98% of our genes with monkeys! Of course, what does make us different from everything else is our human ability to think rationally, that is, to reason.

So, based on all the knowledge we've gathered thus far, it is not so farfetched to also speculate that this present existence in this present configuration is not our only existence and that there is a life hereafter; a life unconstrained by time and space. Another aspect to consider is what we call 'intuition'. As we now know, each particle in the universe has at one time or another been shared with everything and everyone else. Therefore, it is perfectly reasonable to believe that these particles continue to interact with each other. We could call these interactions intuitive, empathic, sympathetic, random or accidental. But, more often than not, these communications are not random, simply because the terms of reference we use—such as intuition, accident, design and random are not well enough understood to provide a contextual understanding of these terms. Some thinkers have a much broader understanding of intuition; for example, Mona Lisa Shultz, in her book *Awakening Intuition* looks upon intuition not so much as a 'gift' bestowed on some of us, but rather as yet another undiscovered dimension with finite rules. According to Roger Highfield, author, in his book the *Arrow of Time, the quest to solve time's greatest mystery,* posits that there are 57 dimensions, of which we know only four. It may well be that, just as intuition may be viewed as its own dimension, so, in a broader context, other conditions such as accidental, or design, random and chaos may also be seen as dimensions, each with their own, as yet, undefined rules. Garrett Lisi, the American theoretical physicist and surfer, is a strong proponent of balance in life, in his case between scientific research and enjoyment of the outdoors is known for "An Exceptionally Simple Theory of Everything," proposing a unified field theory based on the E_8 Lie group, a perfectly symmetrical 248-dimensional object and according to Lisi, the structure that underlies everything in our universe. It took a combined assault of 18 mathematicians from around the world more than four years, to provide the mathematical solution to E8. Who knows, right? Although this object was first discovered in the 19th century, there is evidence that it could contain the structure of the cosmos. The confounding thing about life comes when you view it from two different vantage points: quantum physics: the theory of the infinitesimally small and Einstein's theory: the theory of the very large. We see that many of the principles from both disciplines and the conclusions we draw from them seem to be at odds with each other. That is, of course, not possible. A good scientist will readily admit that what can be proven in one discipline cannot be disputed by the other discipline. So we need to find the common ground between them. Is it a structure made up of a number of elements in either discipline? No it is not a structure because in either discipline it is a process that evolves. This solution seems to make the most sense since from this vantage point it starts out being something that can evolve into something else and one does not contradict the other. If, however, Einstein's work is in violation, it has severe consequences for the use of quantum systems as precise atomic clocks and they will fail to be time dilated, he predicts.

Solution to the entanglement conundrum (Same coin but opposite sides)

1. The quantum state: If we view our self as the observed particle then in the quantum state we are an evolving particle (beings in a progressive state) as in the first tense (I)

2. In the classical state: (Einstein's state of relativity) we are a particle (conscious observant to the state of evolvement) as if in the third tense (He)

Neither is in contravention with the other but betrays two separate observances of the same thing.

WHAT IN THE WORLD?

Time is energy that moves in all directions at once, through the entire energy spectrum and in all known frequencies. It moves so fast that all events, past, present and future co-exist here. That is why, when you ask, whether we affect the events in time or not, that the answer to that question is an emphatic yes and no, since all events already exist. There is no beginning and no end to it. We are part of it but we do not affect it. The events that we think will affect the outcome of time, in reality are mere miniscule slices that in no way matter in the outcome of time's pre-ordained path. It is pre-ordained by an entity that we believe exists but do not know of. It is not one that we can see anyways. It is one that we are told came before everything and set the stage for our progressive evolvement from stage to stage. It is our sense of reality that makes us think that we are affecting the destiny of time because perception of reality is our reality. A strange phenomenon about time is how we measure it. Thanks to Albert Einstein and Henri Poincaré who both claimed, unlike Newton, that time is not absolute but relative. They fundamentally changed our concept of time forever and as we know through Einstein famous formula E=MC2 that time is measured as mass times the square root of the speed of light. So it is that we cannot separate time from space. Hence we can make time what we want it to be and by doing so we believe that our interaction with it changes events. In effect, all we can do in time is affect a tiny strand of it; that very strand that we seem to occupy in space. It is but an exceedingly tiny and slowed down version of the fearsome energy in the multi-verse. In other words the entire energy stream of time is not accessible by us and interaction with the entire spectrum is thus impossible. That is in itself significant since that makes the interaction possible in a very, very large wave form, so large in fact, that it slows down time enough so that we can be a participant in it as a witness to certain events; its cause and effect. The larger the time wave is the slower the time moves. It is the only occasion in our eternal existence that we are enabled to not only participate in the events of time but also to play some part in the outcome, be it ever so infinitesimal. The part that confounds us is: What makes time slow down so that it feels as if we're going through a gooey sticky mass? What is the substance or particle that slows it down that enables us to have an observable and participatory vantage point? Furthermore, it is true that your own experiences of life and those that affect your life's progress are those of your own making. Let us consider this question: Can we measure our impact on the outcome of time. Looking from the outside in, all that you can discern is this tremendous energy without a beginning, middle or end. If we were to jump into this maelstrom in order to affect the outcome of time where would we jump in? There is no way to randomly jump in. The best that we can do is to pull away a tiny strand of this energy and interact with it in some way. So what you do and what you think is that your interaction affects not the entire time energy spectrum, but a miniscule part thereof. What you do is insignificant as it relates to the overall outcome. What we do has virtually no impact on the outcome and all that we can do is to unravel the mysteries of existence by discovering the cure for breast cancer for example; this will impact on a great number of people and therefore leave an indelible mark in time. That is how we can all contribute to the greater good and earn our place in "Heaven". All that we can say about time is that it is what it is. Any moment in time that you think is a moment is just your way of trying to derive a sense of involvement with it. We do have an impact in time, but not in the way you might think. First of all, in large measure the big discoveries that we make in man's destiny and the fulfillment of that destiny is already mapped out. In other words these earthshaking destiny shaping occurrences are meant to happen and thus impacts in the way the entire human destiny is meant to play out. That is the predestination component of time. It would be strange indeed if they were meant to happen and they didn't. It's like connecting the dots in the time map and all of a sudden another gate opens. Don't misunderstand; great discoveries that help unravel the mysteries of the universe are exactly that; great earthshaking discoveries. They shape human destiny, as they were meant to happen simply because all of time is already mapped: past present and future. You might be interested in the fact that the relativity of time allows for many different outcomes beside the one that you are experiencing. So it stands to reason that there exist parallel universes to this one where different outcomes are the result. What is meant to happen in the universe you experience will happen and no other results are possible.

Our own interaction with time and its subsequent results is based in frequencies and wavelengths. It is our ability to operate on a set frequency in time that lets us interact with other beings and things that operate in the same frequency range. An example of frequency lengths we can operate in are very short time frequencies, such as a micro channel frequencies such as: if you were a hobbyist flying remote airplanes or remote cars, the frequencies to control these toys are very short, so that you only control the car and the airplane and not affect the things beyond their range. And so it is with time: at the micro-channel level your impact is on the things and events surrounding you, but when it comes to larger events such as natural phenomena like earthquakes and tsunamis your actions, no matter how heroic, cannot prevent these events from happening. There are billions upon billions of events in time that neither affect you nor change the course of your destiny because the universe or multiverse are just too big and simply because they operate on a myriad of frequencies that are too short to affect you. Let's say, how ever, that these events did impact upon your life, their influence would be so infinitesimal that you might not even know that they happened. Our understanding of cause and effect, that is to say: what you do has a reverberating effect on everything else is only marginally true since your sphere of influence is finite and limited to things and people within your frequency range and it does dissipate into the limitless expanse of time and space. The purpose during our sojourn here is to gather the knowledge and necessary capacity to aid each other onto a path in which it sets the stage for a more peaceful humane existence that is based on principles of conduct which ennobles us rather than the path we find ourselves on today; a path of moral decay and an uncertain future. Remember the theory of multiple universes. This is your universe and the one where what you do has an impact. There are other universes where what you do has not the same impact. And you can only exist and experience, that is to say; see the results of your actions and those around you in your own universe. You probably wonder if there is a different and unique universe for every human being, right? The answer to that is yes, I think. Don't worry about it, you'll understand it one day, or maybe not. Just remember why you're here. This then is your mission and the mission of everyone on earth for the progression of the collective soul and to achieve the goal of your own souls' desire: that is to become a part of the Creative Force.

THE POWER OF INTENTION

"You are what your deepest desire is.
As your desire is, so is your intention.
As your intention is, so is your will.
As your will is, so is your deed.
As your deed is, so is your destiny."

~ Upanishads

"The winds of grace are blowing –
it is you who must raise your sails."

Rabindranath Tagore

We are part of a process of events that will shape us to what we want to become. Appreciate, that you and everyone else are a work in progress. You are part of a complex system in the universe that keeps evolving. That is why it is so difficult to actually comprehend who you really are. When you look at your life in this realm, you cannot fathom the end product of you; the parts, more often than not, don't give you clues about your final destination. We know, however, that as God-fearing beings, what our mission in life is, from the guidance we receive from God's Messengers. We accept, with a great deal of faith, that if we are obedient we will become what we were meant to become and wind up in the place where we are meant to be. Since we are but one miniscule component in the ever-changing energy spectrum it is impossible to conjecture from it what the end product, if there is an end product, will be. I am going through but one stage of an ever-changing, ever-evolving process of existence and what part is uniquely me and what parts are common, I have yet to determine. There is another important component that we don't talk about very much because we don't really understand its implication and that is, free will. We have the ability to choose. Rather than be led by chance and circumstance we can exercise the "Power of Intention." In ancient Sanskrit the Upanishads explains it thus: The Power of Intention means that: "You are what your deepest desire is. As your desire is, so is your intention. As your intention is, so is your will. As your will is, so is your deed. As your deed is, so is your destiny."

Intention is the starting point of every spiritual path. It is the force that fulfills all of our needs,

Whether for money, relationships, spiritual awakening, or love. Intention generates all the

Activities in the universe. Everything that we can see – and even the things we cannot, are an expression of intention's infinite organizing power.

As the ancient Indian sages observed thousands of years ago, our destiny is shaped by the

Deepest level of our intention and desire. Once we plant the seed of an intention in the

Fertile ground of pure potentiality, our soul's journey unfolds automatically, as naturally

As a bulb becomes a tulip an embryo becomes a child.* (*The Chopra Center's Namaste e-newsletter, October 2008)

Your intention is very much influenced by your intensity, your will, your vision, your capacity and your motivating influence.

If it is your intention is to climb Mt. Everest, you'll need tons and tons of motivation, but that's not enough, you'll need tons and tons of capacity. Do you have what it takes?

Practice every day for months and months to build up your endurance. Then you need to visualize, in your mind, ascending the top of the mountain. Do this time and again; see every rock, obstacle, outcropping and crevice. Commit it to memory so that you can, theoretically, scale the mountain with your eyes closed. After all that, you may be ready to tackle the mountain. You may not achieve your goal but at least you have the power of your intention. Get it? As a created being I am created with the unique ability to make choices; free will is crucial to my maturation, as you have said so many times, and even though destiny has me on a path that gave me birth and unequivocally leads me to the end of life here, I can control the events in my life. That coupled with intention lets me do whatever I want to do. Love and empathy, are the necessary ingredients for living a good life. I now know what the recipe is. It's quite simple. Throughout the ages God has counselled us, and all His Messengers have repeated the same simple ground rule: The defining principle that resonates throughout all of man's history; Live your life by the Golden Rule. In Zoroastrianism: Nature only is good when it shall not do to another whatever is not good for its own self. Whatever is disagreeable to yourself do not do unto others.

In Hinduism: This is the sum of all righteousness: Deal with others as you would yourself be dealt by. Do nothing to your neighbour that you would not have him do to you after.

In Buddhism: A clansman should treat his friends and familiars as he treats himself and should be as good as his word. Hurt not others in ways that you yourself would find hurtful.

In Judaism: Love your fellow as you love yourself. What is hateful to you, do not do to your neighbour.

In Christianity: Thou shalt love thy neighbour as thyself. Do to others what you would have them do to you, for this sums up the law and the Prophets.

In Islam: Wish for others what you wish for yourself. None of you is a believer until he desires for his brother what he desires for himself. Hurt no one so that no one may hurt you.

In the Bahá'í Faith: Choose thou for thy neighbour that which thou choosest for thyself. Wish not for others what you wish not for yourself.

The Golden Rule redefines all our humanity, our compassion for others and our common will to help one another. It is the only thing that will guarantee man's continued existence.

Why that should be an epiphany at this time is a question I must answer in this manner: Just as it is impossible, in this life, to walk through a closed door into another room, it is, for the same reason, impossible to learn what we must in this life without trusting the methods of learning that are needed to acquire the knowledge necessary to enter into "Heaven." These methods are, the belief in a Greater Entity and the applied disciplines of prayer and meditation. Consequently we must apply our acquired knowledge.

When you arise in the morning give thanks for the food and for the joy of living. If you see no reason for giving thanks, the fault lies only in yourself. Abuse no one and no thing, for abuse turns the wise ones to fools and robs the spirit of its vision.

When it comes your time to die, be not like those whose hearts are filled with the fear of death, so that when their time comes they weep and pray for a little more time to live their lives over again in a different way. Sing your death song and die like a hero going home.

~ Chief Tecumseh (Poem featured in the movie: Act of Valour)

RECOMMENDED READING LIST

REFERENCES

Berger, P. L. and T. Luckmann 1989: The Social Construction of Reality: A Treatise in the Sociology of Knowledge, Anchor Books, Garden City, NY. ISBN 0-385-05898-5

Blackmore Susan: Consciousness, A very short Introduction: Oxford University Press Inc. New York, 2005, ISBN 978-0-19-280585-0

Bloom Allan: The Republic of Plato, Basic Books a division of The Perseus Books Group ISBN 0-465-06934-7

Close Frank: Nothing: A Very Short Introduction: Oxford University Press, 2009, ISBN: 9780199225866

Davies Paul, The Mind of God: Simon & Schuster 1992. ISBN: 0-671-68787-5

Egginton William: The Philosopher's Desire. Publisher, Stanford University Press 2001, ISBN 978-0-8047-5600-6

Ferguson Kitty: Stephen Hawking: A Quest for a Theory of the Universe. 1992, Bantam Paperback ISBN: 0-553-40507-1

Fife Bruce: The Detox Book: Piccadilly Books, Ltd., 1997 ISBN 0-941-59932-9

Hawking, Stephen (1988): A Brief History of Time, Bantam Books. ISBN 0-553-38016-8

Howe Micheal J.A.: Genius Explained, Cambridge University Press 2001, ISBN-13 9780521008495

Hughes, Robert; Heaven and Hell in Western Art, Publisher, Stein and Day, New York 1968

Jung Carl. G. The Undiscovered Self. Publisher Penguin Books 2006, ISBN 0-451-21860-4

Krauss, Lawrence M.: A Universe From Nothing, Atria paperback, a division of Simon & Schuster Inc. 2012, ISBN 978-1-4516-2446-5

Momen Moojan: The Phenomenon of Religion, Oneworld Publications 1999. ISBN 1-85168-161-2

Oz Mehmet and Roizen, F. Michael: You Staying Young, Simon and Shuster Publisher, New York, ISBN-13 978-0-7432-9256-6

Sachs Joe, Translation of Aristotle Nicomachean Ethics, Focus Publications an R Pullins Company, Newburyport MA, ISBN 1-58510-035-8

Schotter, A. (1981), The Economic Theory of Social Institutions. Cambridge University Press, Cambridge.

Schultz, Mona Lisa, Awakening Intuition. Three Rivers Press, New York 1998, ISBN 0-609-80424-3

Siegel Daniel J., The Developing Mind, The Guilford Press, Second edition 2015, ISBN 97814625206

Tolle Eckhart, The Power of Now: Namaste Publishing and New World Library, Novato California 1997, ISBN 1-57731-480-8

Wolf Fred Alan, Toben Bob: Space-Time and Beyond. Publisher: E P Dutton; May 1982: ISBN-13: 978-0525477105

Periodicals and Internet research sources:

Bisson, M.S., A. Nowell, C. Kordova, R. Kalchgruber and M. al-Nahar: Human evolution at the crossroads: An archaeological survey in Northwest Jordan. Near Eastern Archaeology, vol. 69, no. 2, 2007.

THE BRAIN: Prepared by: The Office of Communications and Public Liaison National Institute of Neurological Disorders and Stroke National Institutes of Health Bethesda, MD 20892 NIH Publication No.02-3440d

Shiga David, New Scientist Magazine, The Cosmos – before the big bang, 28 April 2007

Plato (360 BC) (Benjamin Jowett translation.) "Timaeus." The Internet Classics Archive. http://classics.mit.edu/Plato/timaeus.html. Retrieved on May 30 2006.

www.ingramcontent.com/pod-product-compliance
Lightning Source LLC
Chambersburg PA
CBHW022008100426
42736CB00041B/1112